Who Cares?

Improving Public Schools Through Relationships and Customer Service

KELLY E. MIDDLETON

&

ELIZABETH A. PETITT

Who Cares? Improving Public Schools Through Relationships and Customer Service

Published by Wheatmark™
610 East Delano Street, Suite 104
Tucson, Arizona 85705 U.S.A.
www.wheatmark.com

International Standard Book Number: 978-1-58736-800-4
Library of Congress Control Number: 2007923268

Contents

Preface

Public education is plagued by the process of critics and proponents sharing ideas about what schools should be. Among the many voices are contemporary educators extolling the virtues of three additional Rs in schools: rigor, relevance, and relationships. The new three Rs accompany and work in concert with the traditional ones. A majority of the states have been focusing their efforts on rigor, relevance, and relationships, with the intent of better preparing students for a competitive, global economy and the rapid change that will accompany their education and future career choices. Rigor and relevance are often embraced on the balance scale as being more important and are addressed more intensely and systematically in schools.

Relationships are often viewed like Cinderella: the stepchild of the trio, with an incidental acknowledgement of relationships' role in students' education. However, as we all know Cinderella became the belle of the ball. We are not advocating making rigor and relevance the sacrificial lambs for relationships. Schools should view developing an intentional focus on cultivating relationships and providing great customer service in schools as the foundational piece for truly making a difference. If this difference follows the pattern it has in our district—Mason County, Kentucky—it will be evidenced in improved student achievement, in reducing gaps among subgroups, in decreasing discipline referrals, and in increasing the number of volunteer hours in schools.

School administrators and classroom teachers are accountable for an increasing number of expectations, which include meeting the needs of more diverse student populations. Within the pages of this book, school leaders will find a description of some of the realities schools face, including increasing scrutiny and competition. We share these realities as a way of building a case for change and the need to focus on relationships. This book contains a variety of resources and ideas to help schools become more intentional in their efforts to develop relationships.

This book is a reminder of several things: why teachers entered their profession, the power they have as teachers, and the growing realization that the various factors impinging upon public education may threaten public education as it currently exists. From the one-room schoolhouse to the large, diverse schools characterizing many of today's districts and states, effective teachers have always known the importance of relationships and high expectations— and their impact on student learning. We offer ideas for intentionally forging and developing relationships to share how teachers and schools can continue to meet the needs of individual learners.

Chapter one addresses the various attacks on public education and challenges schools to examine their practices, particularly as they relate to customer service and forming relationships among students, parents, and the community. This chapter reminds the reader that public education is a lightning rod for criticism and that we must begin the process of educating ourselves about the competition and seek to become more customer friendly. It also provides information that can be used to "sell" the importance of moving toward more customer-oriented schools. Some of the scenarios and information in chapter one may be disconcerting, but the chapter is geared toward identifying some of the strangleholds that exist in public education without assigning blame. Beyond the problems and beyond chapter one is a plan for helping public schools loosen the strangleholds and begin a rewarding journey. This journey is characterized by building quality customer service programs and by developing better relationships among school personnel, students, and parents. These relationships translate into improved academic achievement for all students and a community that sees itself as a true partner with its public schools.

Everything rises and falls with leadership, and chapter two

outlines the importance of leadership within the framework of customer service and making connections with students. It encourages the importance of initiating a dialogue about practices in this regard. Chapter two provides examples of how a school leader can cultivate a customer-focused attitude among school personnel. Chapter three continues this idea by focusing on ways schools can obtain data about their customer service practices and begin to differentiate between perception and reality. This chapter provides the school leader with a variety of ways to collect data about the culture and the practices of the school from the perspective of the "customer."

Just as education is plagued with many competing voices, it is also plagued by the deafening silence of students who often seem disconnected from and disenfranchised by the educational process. Chapter four emphasizes the critical role of the teacher in forming and sustaining relationships with students and delineates various practices to this end. It embraces home visits by teachers and administrators and outlines various ideas for relationship building.

Chapter five illustrates that, in order to truly be effective, the customer service initiative must permeate every aspect of the school and must be the responsibility of every employee. We offer suggestions relating to the role of each employee of the school, from the custodian to the bus driver, for districts seeking to develop expectations. A relationship hierarchy captures how this initiative can evolve at different levels and create a culture of caring and making connections. Chapter five has specific customer service tips that can be used for training purposes or as guides for school leaders, teachers, and staff as they develop their approach to customer service and making connections.

Finally, we present the reader with a list of ten best practices that mirror the customer service efforts of the business world. There is often apprehension when using business as a model for efforts within public education. This is understandable, since educational professionals are not manufacturing a product, but shaping human lives. However, the essence of any successful business is building and sustaining relationships with customers, and schools can learn from business practices as they seek to connect with students, parents, and the community. Public schools are also experiencing "competition" for students, funds, and services. The goal of these ten practices is improving customer service and making connections to insure our customers know we care about them and want them to succeed. The key question that frames this list is: What does great customer service look like in public schools?

Chapter six asks educators to contemplate their practices and look for ways to redefine what has traditionally been done in schools in the area of customer service and relationships.

The authors are administrators in Mason County, Kentucky, a school district of 2,700 students; these initiatives are "home-grown" and are being incorporated throughout the system and with all staff members. The practices outlined in the chapters have been implemented in grades K–12 in a district that has a free and reduced lunch population of approximately 60% at the elementary level and 50% district wide. There is an African-American population of around 12% and a special-education population of about 15%. Teachers are making connections with students from pre-school through high school, with results that include reducing gaps while increasing student achievement.

Mason County Schools have progressed from one of the lowest CATS assessment scores in the state to scoring in the top 15% of Kentucky districts. Our schools have been recognized by the Kentucky Department of Education, and our intermediate school was recently named a Title I Distinguished School. We hold our teachers and staff in high esteem, because we know it's people, not programs, that make a difference in the classroom. Mason County teachers demonstrate a true commitment to students while maintaining high expectations. Customer service initiatives are having a positive impact on all facets of the schools, from student achievement to school culture. Teachers in Mason County know the students they teach, have high expectations for each one, and hold their students accountable.

Acknowledgments

To all those who plant seeds of possibilities in the lives of others:
This book is a tribute to the power of what grows from those seeds. We offer special thanks to those who planted seeds of possibilities for us, and we challenge ourselves and others to continually "pay it forward."

To our colleagues, who make us accountable and promote our growth:
This book is a testament to the impact of your conversations, your encouragement, and the value of teamwork.

To our friends, who embrace and share a passion for life, work, and our time together:
This book is a reminder of your importance in our personal and professional lives and validates the significance of real relationships.

To our families, who honor us with their unconditional love and reassurance:
This book honors your sacrifices, embraces your love, and offers gratitude to you for teaching us some of life's most important lessons.

To all those individuals who go above and beyond the call of duty in making a difference in the lives of students:
This book is an expression of gratitude for your labor of love, your unselfish nature, and your determination to see students succeed.

To all Mason County teachers and staff:

This book demonstrates what can be done when individuals reach out, make connections, and put students first. This book represents what can happen when people look for ways to make things happen, instead of offering excuses for why ideas won't work. This book salutes your efforts and dedication.

Chapter One:

If Public Education Were a Stock, Would You Invest?

D*ear Educator:*
For now, I have chosen your school for my child. The education my child receives and how my child and I are treated at your school are critical to me. You are part of my customer service experience. I just want you to know that I expect you to act always in the best interest of the students at your school.

When I come to your school office or to your classroom, or when I call your school, I expect to be treated well by the people who assist me. I will also judge your school by much more than how the teacher or office staff respond to me during my visit. I am one of those concerned parents who will analyze everything. I look. I ask questions. I make judgments. Is the school clean and well maintained? Are best practices occurring in the classrooms? Is my child progressing as he should? Is my child treated with respect by caring professionals on a daily basis? Do the professionals at this school know the specific gifts of my child?

My list of questions goes on and on and eventually touches all areas of the school and its personnel, from the janitor to the principal. Whether you know it or not, you are in the customer service business. What you and the school do impacts me in some way.

I'll bet you're saying to yourself, "I wish this parent would move and let us do our thing. After all, we are the professionals." I can understand that attitude. However, let me remind you that even though you may never know me personally and, in fact, may never even see me, you shouldn't dismiss me and treat me as though my thoughts and concerns are unimportant. Please remember that I am the reason your school ex-

ists. I and thousands of others like me are the reason you have a job. I want what every customer wants: a great educational experience for my child and myself. By keeping focused on the most important thing, I will send my future children and grandchildren to your school. I will speak positively about your school and even may help recruit private- or homeschooled children to come back to your school. If you can't or don't live up to your part of the bargain because you don't think schools are in the business of customer service, then I have no other choice but to go somewhere else.

I believe educators often think that parents do not have any choices other than public schools. However, that is a faulty assumption, because I can choose from a multitude of private schools—or, like many other parents, I just might choose to homeschool my child. I am not writing this letter to threaten or to try to intimidate the school. I believe from the bottom of my heart that we both want the same thing. I will end this letter by sharing that as a customer, I am highly critical, because the product you offer and the services you provide impact the most important aspect of my life: my children. The choice is yours ... and mine!

Your Customer

Some might be offended by this letter, while others would simply be inclined to dismiss it as an attempt to "strong-arm" the school into letting parents influence the way schools do business. But the question that resounds is, "Are schools doing business in a customer-friendly and inviting manner and reaping the benefits—or does anyone even care?"

Think about the role of education from a customer service perspective. Think about the teachers in your life who believed in you, planted seeds of possibilities, and made you envision things for yourself that you never imagined. Effective educators have always cared about students, articulated high expectations, and provided support to insure success. Effective educators have always "known" their students and worked with the home, the parents, and the community to help their students. They may not have called it customer service, but the end result or product was a powerful connection and a desire not to disappoint. However, it seems that in a fast-paced society that is constantly changing, and in an era where, often, the bottom line is test scores, relationships and making connections become casualties. The problem is that often the efforts of these effective educators are isolated examples instead of a system-wide focus. If schools are not customer service oriented, and if each staff member is not involved in making connections with students, the question we should be asking ourselves in the face of increased competition is: "How much longer can we last?"

Ignorance or Arrogance?

It seems that public school employees are marching blindly toward a goal, and no one sees the writing on the wall: the mistrust and disconnectedness of public education from all facets of society. One might even call it the death of public education, with various stakeholders eulogizing the current plight of public schools.

Do we in public education know the ramifications of our own ignorance? Are we aware of all the factions competing for education funds, all the voices shouting that they can do it better, all those who perpetuate a certain ideology contrary to the basic concept that schools should do what's best for students? Are we aware of all the policymakers and decision-makers who negotiate for public trust in a process critical to the survival of any society?

Maybe we are so caught up in the demands of the profession that we are unaware that public education seems to be moving closer and closer to the edge of a cliff. We may find ourselves facing the same dilemma of other big businesses. The "Montgomery Ward Saga" might provide a reference point for those in education.

Montgomery Ward: A Chronological Story

Year	Event
1872	• First dry-good mail-order catalog established by Aaron Montgomery Ward

1875	• Company coined phrase "Satisfaction guaranteed or your money back"
1883	• Company grew from a one-page catalog in 1872 to a 240-page catalog *(from 163 to 10,000 items)*
1900	• Company generated $8.7 million in sales
1926	• Company opened first retail store
1928	• Company operated 244 stores, which grew to 531 the following year
1930	• Company declined offer to join with Sears
1939	• Company introduced *Rudolph the Red-Nosed Reindeer*; Sold six million copies of book
1985	• Company discontinued catalog sales • Company focused on specialty store strategy
1991	• Company resumed catalog sales
1997	• Company filed for Chapter 11 Bankruptcy
2000	• Company closed 250 stores in thirty states *Employees notified by faxes, e-mails, and conference calls *Employees surprised by closings *37,000 employees lost their jobs

(Irvine, 2006, p. 1–12)

Much was written about the demise of Montgomery Ward and the circumstances that contributed to it. Karen Talaski of the Detroit *News* wrote, "Once a retail mainstay, department stores are struggling to show their relevance in a marketplace dominated by discounters and specialty stores. Stores that ruled the retail landscape now face closures, bankruptcy, even extinction." She continues by quoting Joe Grillo, a retail analyst who shared, "Retail is about evolution. It's about new concepts coming and attracting the customer, and taking its marketing share from existing operators." (Talaski, 2001, p. 1). This idea is supported by a colleague of Talaski of the *Detroit News* who shared the perspective of a owner of a retail establishment in an article, "Rethinking Shopping." Ricardo Thomas quotes Monty Mitzfield, "We're all dinosaurs. It's just a matter of who's going to be the best dinosaur" (Thomas, 2001, p.1).

Could what happened with Montgomery Ward happen in public education, or is it already occurring? Are public schools dinosaurs who are failing to change, failing to show their relevance and are public schools being out-maneuvered by aggressive competitors? There appear to be some uncanny parallels between public education and Montgomery Ward. Consider the following:

- Cornering the market

  o Montgomery Ward and public schools operate on the premise that they have a corner on the market. Both seem to be victims of their own visions of success. Did Montgomery Ward or does public education believe in the power of its competitors? Why should public schools worry about these parallels? This question can be answered succinctly: decreasing funding and increasing competition. Although the funds appropriated for public education seem to be increasing, the fallacy of this assumption is revealed by analyzing the percentage of state budgets that are set aside for public schools. Often, these percentages show a decrease in the total budget for public schools. Couple this trend with the fact that there are increasing demands from private and home schools for their piece of the pie, and it appears that public schools' corner of the market may be eroding more than one would care to admit.

- Employees unaware

o   Montgomery Ward employees were shocked to learn that the company was going out of business. Anece Rich, a twenty-eight-year employee said, "I'm just devastated … They took care of us best they could" (Irvine, 2007, p. 2). An "it can't happen to us" mentality existed among the employees. Is that attitude prevalent among public school educators? Mike Antonucci (2001) cites a survey by the National Education Association of the membership that indicates that the answer to this question is yes. This survey indicates that "a remarkable 61% of members do not consider it important for the union to speak out on the issue of school vouchers" (p. 1). This finding may suggest that public school teachers are not aware and do not feel threatened by the concept of vouchers. Funding follows students. Students equal jobs—either the addition or loss of positions. Could public school teachers experience some of the same shock as Montgomery Ward employees?

- Failed to change

o   Not only did Montgomery Ward fail to change, but—unlike its more flexible competitors, Target and Wal-Mart—the company seemed unsure of what changes to make to address its customers' concerns. There were layers and layers of bureaucracy before any changes could be made. Public education today can also be portrayed as anti-change, with a bureaucratic structure that rivals any business or government agency.

Is public education suffering from some of the same problems that plagued Montgomery Ward? How aware are school personnel at all levels about the competing factions for public school monies and students? How informed are educators about the trends in school financing at the state level? How in sync are public school employees with the attitudes of the public and the criticisms that are continually being leveled against public schools? Public education cannot afford to follow in the footsteps of Montgomery Ward, where the people working within the organization were unaware the company was walking down the wrong path. The company's destination left these people jobless.

When analyzing the demise of Montgomery Ward, one cannot help but wonder if assumptions made about the future of the company were based on arrogance. Were those involved so confident about their efforts and so content with their many "firsts" that they felt they didn't have to worry about the competition? As one considers plausible explanations about why Montgomery Ward didn't change to challenge its competitors and why education is not changing to answer its own challenges, one must confront the idea of arrogance. An Arabian proverb that conveys the dangers associated with this characteristic holds that "Arrogance diminishes wisdom." Maybe the education profession needs to determine to what degree the word *arrogance* encapsulates the problems inherent in public education.

Let's ask ourselves the following questions:

- Do we automatically assume that just because public education has existed in its present form for decades, it will continue to do so?

- Do we believe that all the negative publicity shared through the media about schools and school employees has no impact on the general public?

- Do we believe that public education is immune to competition?

- Do we believe that there will always be widespread support for public education?

- Do we even care about the contemporary trends in education?

- Do we realize the impact of individuals within our profession who put job security above the needs of the students we teach?

- Do we understand the significance of not playing the "blame game," not making excuses, or even the perils of being content with the status quo?

One might expect the education profession to be one of the wisest, one that would embrace practices that would lead to improved performance. However, the current state of affairs within the profession is sobering. Attacks on public education, national legislation that will eventually result in the majority of schools not meeting national goals, an increasing population of homeschooled and privately schooled children, mounting political pressure for vouchers—the walls seem to be closing in on public schools. Whether it is arrogance or a milder case of complacency, public educators can no longer afford to look the other way.

It's Now or Never

"What I see is, the people running [the public schools] don't have any sense of urgency ... It's too late for you to say, 'Trust me. Give me time.' If my children are already in school, I don't have the time to give you" (Caire, 2002, p. 38). This comment by Roberta Kitchen, a mother whose four children attend private schools in Cleveland, underscores an important call to action. This call to action cannot occur some time in the future, and it cannot wait for the next national school reform movement. If things are to change, we must have a sense of urgency that guides action.

Charlie T. Jones, a motivational speaker and author of leadership materials, conveys the essence of a sense of urgency. He writes:

The fires of greatness in our heart can be kept aglow only after we develop a sense of urgency and importance for what we are doing. I mean a sense of urgency to the extent that we feel it is a matter of life and death ... If you don't believe this, talk to anyone that has lost a sense of urgency of getting things done and has been drifting in complacency, mediocrity, and failure.

The public's patience is running short, and parents are concerned about their children receiving a quality education. Schools should be having conversations about the problems confronting the educational system and what competitors are doing to create a more welcoming environment. Our customers—students and their parents—are making choices that take them away from public education. A sports euphemism extols the virtues of having a good defense in order to have a good offense. Public school supporters must be proactive by being aware of the factors that attract increasing support for alternatives for public education. Are public schools reflecting to see what we are doing to create problems, erect barriers, or perpetuate the status quo? Are public schools concerned about the parent who wrote the letter at the beginning of this chapter and what might cause him to leave the public schools? Being proactive is predicated on a knowledge of the facts, even if these facts prevent one from getting a good night's sleep.

Four Indicators that Public Education Stock Is on a Downward Spiral

A survey of trends in public education and professional literature depicts several leading indicators that should be red flags for proponents of public education. Public educators go to work every day thinking that education is a "blue chip" stock. The truth is that an investor in public education might issue a stop-loss order asking the broker to sell if things became any worse. It might appear that "public education stock" is headed for a crash. One day we may realize that what we thought were harmless and isolated problems within the field of education are actually indicators of widespread issues that are eating away at the foundations of quality, customer-oriented public education.

Organizational expert and management consultant, Jim Collins and his colleagues have researched various organizations to identify the leverage points that distinguish great organizations from good ones. As he states in his book *Good to Great*, people must confront the brutal facts about their organization if they are to grow and thrive and not become a "sad remnant" of a recent past (Collins, 2001, p. 69). Brutal facts refer to the information and knowledge that is often difficult for an organization to acknowledge and systematically address. Some organizations choose to ignore or explain away data or information. Great organizations are not only aware of the data about themselves, but they immediately work to develop a plan of action to address the concerns. They have faith that problems can be solved.

As one examines the following four indicators, the question that begs asking is: What do these "brutal facts" mean for public education?

Indicator #1: Increase in Number of and Support for Private Schools

Private schools are attracting a larger segment of the general population. Whether they are prestigious schools that cater to an elite population or schools with a religious affiliation, private schools tripled the growth rate of public schools (6.7% versus 2.3%) between 1999 and 2003 (Feller, 2004, p. A11). Some parents, politicians, private sector members and organizations are pursuing and advocating the financial support of additional options under the banner of the "School Choice Movement." Resources are being appropriated to alternative educational structures, diverting needed monies from public education. For instance, from 1991 to 1998, the state of Ohio supported private schools at a price tag of $1.1 billion, more than it allocated on "refurbishing its public schools," $1 billion (McDonald, 2002, p. 36).

Could you ever envision Wal-Mart giving part of its proceeds to K-Mart? Would Burger King ever bus some of its customers to McDonalds? Would you invest in a company that helped finance its competitors? Yet, that is the reality for public schools that receive federal funds. Financial support of private schools is at the expense of public schools.Public schools must seek out private school and homeschool leaders, explaining the different funding options and requirements, and asking them to indicate if they wish to participate. If the private school chooses to operate within the parameters attached to the federal educational programs, a formula is used to divert the appropriate resources from the public school to the private school. It is the responsibility of the public school to monitor the program, to communicate to the private schools, and to complete and file all the necessary paperwork.

Beyond a growing financial commitment in resources and dollars to private schools is a growing acceptance of the role of private schools in what some believe should be a competitive market for students. The National Center for Education Statistics conducted an analysis of private schools, resulting in some interesting findings. Consider the following:

- Private schools generally have smaller enrollments and a lower student/teacher ratio than public school counterparts (13:1 versus 16:1—and in 36% of private schools, the ratio is lower than 10:1).

- Private schools are less likely to enroll students who are minorities, who speak English as a second language, or who are eligible for free or reduced school lunches.

- Private school teachers report feeling more influential in the school's instructional practices and policies than public school teachers.

- Private school teachers report greater satisfaction with their work than public school teachers (66% versus 54%), vis-à-vis such issues as cooperation, collegiality, and parental support (42% versus 16%).

- Private school teachers express more support for and positive appraisals of the school management than public school teachers.

- Eighty percent of public school principals conveyed that teaching basic literacy skills was one of their top three goals, compared to only 51% of private school principals suggesting that private school principals believe their schools have a stronger foundation in literacy .

- Test scores for private school students tend to be higher than public school students in the areas of reading, math, and science, with private school graduates completing advanced coursework in a minimum of three academic subject areas.

- Private school students are twice as likely to complete at least a minimum of a bachelor's degree by their midtwenties (Alt & Peter, 2002, p. 1–35).

Initial perusal of this information might lead one to the conclusion that private schools seem more customer oriented. Public schools need to determine why we are not doing some of the same things that customers find attractive in private schools. Is it ignorance, arrogance, or a lack of leadership?

As one can surmise from this analysis, those who embrace private schools as a better choice for students than public schools have a number of arguments they might present to any detractors. One can debate potential influences on the outcomes for private schools, such as selective enrollment practices, greater parental support, and a more diverse, experiential background. In fact, *Education Week* (May 4, 2005) cites a research study that even provides data to counter the argument that private school students outperform public school students on measures of achievement. The authors concluded that public school students outperform private school students when accounting for socioeconomic status, race, and disability (Lubienski & Lubienski, 2004, p. 22). Yet the findings of this research study did not receive front-page coverage or widespread celebration from government officials. The findings remained buried, except for some coverage in educational journals and publications. Even with the positive results of these academic comparisons, it is difficult to circumvent the general public's belief that private schools are better than public schools.

Could public school teachers be their own worst enemy when it comes to the growth of private schools? As humans, do we react to what people say or to what they do? When you go to your dentist and he recommends the dental products he uses, do you find yourself purchasing those same brands?

What do these questions have to do with the public and private school debate? Maybe a headline from a *Washington Times* article by Joel Brondos (2004) captures the essence of these questions: "Public Schools No Place for Teachers' Kids." The article states that public school teachers are twice as likely as nonteachers to send their own children to private schools. Consult the following table to compare the percentage of public school teachers who send their children to private schools in a sampling of some of the nation's major cities.

City	% of Public School Teachers Sending Child to Private School
Philadelphia	44%
Cincinnati	41%
Chicago	39%
Baltimore	35%
New York	33%

(Brondos, 2004, p. 1–2).

One might find a correlation to the crime rate within these cities, but that does not negate the fact that many public educators choose to send their children to private schools. In a 2004 poll, the general public felt that the teacher was more believable than others (78%) when it came to rating school quality (Hunter, 2004). The bottom line is that actions speak louder than words and the general public believes teachers know what a good school looks like.

By enrolling their own children in private schools, public school teachers communicate a belief that private schools have better discipline, more rigorous coursework, and an atmosphere more conducive to learning. This sends a powerful message to the general population. If public schools are not good enough for the children whose parents teach there, and if those most invested in public education are making a different choice, the message is clear: public schools are not good enough for parents who are truly concerned about their child's education!

Growing support for private schools is also evidenced by the practices of a group of decision-makers who are the ultimate power brokers. George Clowes, managing editor of *School Reform News* maligned members of Congress for not supporting school choice after reviewing results from a survey conducted by the Heritage Foundation. This survey found that 49% of senators and 40% of representatives responding had chosen private schools for one or more of their own children. In addition, the survey revealed that Congressional members with school-aged children served on committees that could impact funding for public education. The survey included the following statistics:

- 61% of Senate Finance Committee members and 57% of Senate Health, Education, Labor, and Pensions Committee members send or have sent their children to private schools.

- 43% of House Ways and Means Committee members chose private schools for their children. (Clowes, 2000, p. 1)

This trend is repeated with other state lawmakers and city officials. State after state, city after city, the same scene is being played out with the same results. Sentiments are best summarized by a former California congressman and the current mayor of Los Angeles, Antonio Villaraigosa who is married to a public school teacher. He shared with the Los Angeles *Times* that "As a parent, no matter how passionate you are about public schools, in the final analysis you're going to do what's best for your children" (Clowes, 2000, p. 2).

Evidently, for some people, doing what's best for their children translates into enrolling them in private school. For those who believe in public education, trying to combat the arguments levied against public schools is an endless battle. For those employed by public schools, it should be a travesty that public schools are not good enough for their own children. Legislators at the state and national level have the power to create a disaster for public educators by supporting school choice and attaching dollars.

Indicator #2: Increase in Homeschool Movement

Private schools are not the only competition for public school support. Home schools are gaining in popularity and have become a big business with an influential advocacy and lobbying effort. Any attempts to "credentialize" homeschooling with regulations, expectations, or teacher qualifications are derailed quickly and effectively. Only one of the fifty states, North Dakota, has any requirement that a homeschool teacher have more than a GED or high school diploma. In fact, qualifications for homeschool teachers are often listed as "none" (Home School Legal Defensive Association, State Laws).

Since 1999, there has been a 29% growth in the number of homeschooled children—1.1 million students (Feller, 2004, p. A11). If you were a retailer and your competition grew by 29%, would you be worried? According to Reich, "Homeschooling is the fastest growing segment of the education market, expanding at a rate of 15% to 20% a year" (Reich, 2002, p. 56). Think about what this means for public education, especially since funding is predicated on school enrollment. Public schools are losing students, resources, and financing at an alarming rate.

The growth of the homeschool movement can be attributed

to a number of factors. What is the appeal of homeschooling to the general public? In some states, it is a way for parents to evade legal action when their child gets in trouble with the school and/or judicial system. Other parents are concerned about the general quality of local public education or have a desire to incorporate religious instruction as an integral aspect of their child's education. For some people, it is a way to insure their child learns in a safe and controlled environment. Others are responding to policymakers' legitimization of the movement, as exemplified by Congress designating an official National Home Education Week in 1999, with recurring celebration of the event on an annual basis. Still others might be swayed by a cursory glance at the academic performance data of homeschool students; students in home schools are scoring fifteen to thirty percentile points above their public school counterparts on standardized achievement tests (Ray, 2002, p. 50–54), a statistic that is questioned and even disputed by other researchers.

In a 2003 National Household Education Survey, parents reported reasons for homeschooling. The three major reasons cited by parents were:

(1) Concern about the environment of the school (31%)

(2) Religious and moral instruction (30%)

(3) Dissatisfaction with academic instruction (16%)

(Feller, 2004, p. A11).

Homeschools offer parents an alternative approach to their child's education. Homeschool parents are even partnering with community organizations or other homeschool parents to provide additional educational experiences beyond the home. Parents feel homeschools offer an ideal way of controlling the variables that may impact their child's learning, allowing an educational experienced tailored to the individual child. In a study by Brian Way of the National Home Education Research Institute, Way answered the question of why parents are choosing to homeschool with three words: "Because it works."

As public schools fall victim to a litany of ailments and the perpetuation of a belief that it is a broken system, the nightmare for public school advocates intensifies. Knowing the facts, understanding the arguments, and listening to the concerns necessitates that we avoid becoming defensive and that we take on the role of offering a better option.

Indicator #3: Teacher Unions and Bureaucracy

As one surveys literature on the growing bureaucracy that permeates education, it is evident that teacher unions have gained support for important issues within the profession—issues that make the profession better and attract quality candidates to the field of teaching. Lowering class size, lobbying for adequate pay, working for health benefits for employees, and promoting the importance of public schools during school choice debates are some of the teacher union efforts that must be applauded.

But even though teacher unions have brought about positive changes, there are those who find that unions have also impeded the changes needed to prevent the stock in public education from dwindling even lower. On the Internet, those arguments are only a couple of mouse clicks away; one can find critics and writers who blame teacher unions for putting barriers in the path of substantive change geared toward improved student achievement.

Is public education about kids or about adults? If you polled the general populace, the response would be overwhelmingly in favor of the kids. However, if you examined policies and practices within government, within unions, and within the field of education, the answer would alarmingly favor adults. Consider the following critiques.

(A) The Job Security Criticism

One of the most debatable beliefs held by union detractors is that the union perpetuates job security to the detriment of some classrooms of students. Every organization, including education organizations, knows that success depends on hiring the best people. Conversely, one must be prepared to make tough personnel decisions when the performance of an employee adversely affects the organization. Imagine that the CEO of a major company evaluates personnel and, after intervening with additional training, finds that the performance of one of the workers remains unsatisfactory. The CEO would decide it was in the best interest of the organization's productivity to terminate the employee. The termination occurs immediately in this scenario. This is often not the case in public schools. Although business, like education must travel some of the same paths related to union issues, the difference is we are dealing with the educational lives of our students. One cannot help but wonder if, certain aspects take on a life of their own, and the end result may not have any resemblance to the original purpose. The issue becomes preventing unsafe and unfair treatment of employees without providing a sanctuary for poor teacher performance.

The educational equivalent of this is a plethora of policies and procedures that impede or delay the ability to terminate an ineffective teacher. Most school districts must notify an employee of a nonrenewal of contract by a specified date prior to end of the school year. This individual will remain on the job until the end of the school year and will often create an uncomfortable working environment. He or she may appeal negative evaluations, and ultimately, in many states, a jury of teaching peers renders a consensus opinion regarding the appeal.

Terry Moe is a Stanford University professor and a senior fellow at Hoover Institution who is regarded as an expert on educational policy, United States political institutions, and organization theory. He has written extensively on school choice, bureaucracy, and education issues. Mr. Moe underscores the fact that teacher unions "are dedicated to protecting the jobs of all members. The rules they insist upon make it virtually impossible for schools to get rid of even the worst teachers, not to mention the ones who are merely mediocre" (Moe, 2005, p. 4).

This idea is supported by other observers and organizations, including Frederick Hess of the American Enterprise Institute and Martin West of the Brookings Institute. They write:

Teachers have been caught sticking children's heads in toilets, reading the newspaper while children gambled in the back of the room, and missing months of school at a stretch, and yet kept their jobs. The New Teacher Project's recent study of five urban districts discovered that only four teachers out of the 70,000 in those districts were terminated for poor performance....Frank Brogan, the former superintendent and education commissioner of Florida, remarks that 'tenure was originally designed to protect the best teachers from wrongful termination. Today it protects the worst teachers from rightful termination (Hess & West, 2005, pp 27-28).

The article continues by citing the comments from union representatives including one from New Jersey who "confessed, I've gone in and defended teachers who shouldn't even be pumping gas" (Hess and West, 2005, p. 28). Experiences and comments such as these demonstrate why it is difficult for some to believe that union motives are intertwined with the students' best interests.

So, is it about kids or about adults? A statement made by Albert Shanker, former president of the American Federation of Teachers, offers a sad commentary to this question. "Teacher unions will start representing children as soon as kids pay union dues," he says (Maranto, 2002, p. 1; Clowes, 2001, p. 1). Unfortunately, when some union leaders share this perspective, their words are piercing and demonstrate a lack of concern for the very reason teacher unions exist: the students. This provides critics of unions with an "I told you so" moment.

It might serve everyone to keep in mind that without students, there would be no teachers; without teachers, no teacher unions. It is incumbent on those in the profession, whatever their roles, to pursue more common-ground approaches to problems in education. Nothing is as one-sided as it may appear to be. A favorite expression captures best the reality of any discussion of two or more sides of an issue: the truth lies somewhere in between.

This is illustrated in an article entitled "Broadening Collective Bargaining," in which author Jennifer Maciejewski related that positive changes can occur. For example, the Cincinnati Federation of Teachers (CFT) bargained with the school district to provide a peer assistance and evaluation program. The article discussed how CFT and other organizations are working to "broaden the scope of bargaining, moving beyond salary and benefits negotiations to tackle issues that improve all aspects of the profession, from teacher quality to the school environment in the name of children" with initiatives such as peer review and assistance teams (Maciejewski, 2007, p. 36).

This concept was supported by William Raabe, director of collective bargaining and member advocacy for the National Education Association. He clearly articulated the positive impact that unions could bring to the table by broadening the scope of collective bargaining.

> Looking at the scope of bargaining is really important because we are focused on creating a great public school for every child ...It's all about having our voice—the people who are working directly with the students—in the room when we're talking about issues that impact the quality of teaching and learning (Maciejewski, 2007, p. 36).

Ms. Maciejewski provides corroborating comments and examples including a statement by the Rochester Teacher's Association president, Adam Urbanski, who maintains that:

> Principals and supervisors used to be reluctant to fire a teacher due to unsatisfactory job performance because it threatened the livelihood of the person.... All too often, teachers would just automatically get satisfactory evaluations.... Now, with

teachers involved in the process, they are proving to be faithful guardians of their own profession and their own standards (Maciejewski, 2007, p. 37).

(B) The "We Elect Our Own Boss" Criticism

Teacher unions influence a number of political activities. One must acknowledge that all unions lobby on behalf of their members. However, the difference within the educational arena centers around the question: Does the emphasis on adult issues come at the expense of student issues?

Simplistically, a board's role is to protect the interests of the investors, to insure that a quality product is being offered, and to forecast possible changes and weather the storms that might negatively impact the business. The interests of the board relate directly to the interests and welfare of the organization.

As one attempts to generalize the educational equivalent of this, the role of teacher unions again comes into play. In many states, school board members are elected, not appointed. Some might postulate that the marriage between teacher unions and political action groups is an enduring one that is, paradoxically, like the fox guarding the henhouse. Former kindergarten teacher and Illinois AFL-CIO president Margaret Blackshere commented, "One of the wonderful things about being a teacher is that you get to help elect your own bosses" (Reeder, 2005, p. 1). "Teacher unions are in the astounding position of being able to determine who sits on local school boards, and thus with whom they will be bargaining" she went on (Moe, 2001, p. 7). One of unions' basic objectives is influencing political races at all levels: local, state, and national. They devote a major part of their budget to political campaigns and lobbying. One survey depicted teacher unions as the number one interest group exercising political influence, a rating that surpassed "business organizations, trial lawyers, doctors, insurance companies, environmentalists, and even state AFL-CIO affiliates" (Moe, 2001, p. 7). Joel Mowbray echoes this sentiment. He writes:

> The National Education Association (NEA), with 2.6 million members, is the nation's largest union and one of the most powerful lobbies in Washington. One of every twelve delegates to the 2000 Democratic Convention was an NEA member—total: 350, a number greater than the entire California delegation. This kind of clout makes it a political kingmaker (Mowbray, 2001, p. 1).

Funding means favor. Favor translates into influencing political decision-making and political races.

Beyond the primary goal of political influence, unions sometime play out the drama of allowing adult issues to upstage student issues. One must determine whether teacher unions' efforts are directed toward enacting work rules and protections, rather than focusing on issues related to students and education. One might argue that, unlike other unions that pursue similar goals for their members, the "product" in education are students, whose success is greatly influenced by the quality of the teacher. Following the money reveals the philosophy adhered to by some union leadership and membership when it comes to selecting who gets to make the decisions and what decisions get made. Decisions equal strict constraints. The intent may be different than the outcome. The end result is like putting a restraining jacket on public schools. Interaction with employees, clear focus on job expectations, and making connections with students cannot be accomplished within a straightjacket mentality. Consider the following list of some of the categories of union rules for teachers from Terry Moe. There are:.

- Rules for assigning teachers to classrooms

- Rules for non-assignment of teachers to playgrounds and lunchrooms

- Rules about how much time teachers can be asked to work after school

- Rules about how much time to plan for classes

- Rules about class schedules

- Rules about number and use of teacher aides

- Rules about teacher involvement in school policy decisions

- Rules about grievances

- Rules about the number of faculty meetings

- Rules about how often teachers are required to meet with parents

(Moe, 2001, p. 3)

There are those who assert the rules that are important to teacher unions, are not geared toward reform and finding solutions to problems. The rules perpetuate a desire to immobilize the organization. Can you imagine a business organization having a rule limiting the number of times employees could meet with a client or customer? It would be difficult to imagine the faces of students who must endure schools that operate on the premise that schools are more about the adults than about doing what's best for all students. Is help after school when a student is struggling with a concept contingent upon a union contract? Must groups of students become casualties in a classroom where the teacher is ineffective? Is that what we truly want for our youth?

C. On Common Ground: Adults Working Together for Students?

Is it about students or about adults? It's ironic that the profession that should be totally child centered often appears to be more about adults, more about politics, and more about operating in isolation than even some businesses. It's ironic that the unions for educational professionals may actually impede student achievement. Harvard professor, Caroline Hoxby's analysis of this phenomena is summarized in the following statement: "The unions are responsible for making the education system much more formal, more complex and impersonal than it would otherwise be. These characteristics tend to undermine school performance" (Moe, 2001, p. 6).

It is our contention that teachers who work in the classroom on a daily basis are staunch believers in the power of caring, and they want to make a difference for the students. It is also our contention that the union has waged many battles that have made a positive impact on the profession. It is always a good practice to look at what critics say, ascertain if there is validity in the statements, and determine any needed changes so students are the number one priority in all our efforts.

One can point fingers at several organizations that put the good of the organization above the good of students. Teachers aren't the only ones who have advocacy groups and organizations. Administrators, school boards, special interest groups within education (special education, gifted/talented, principals, superintendents, instructional supervisors, transportation, pupil personnel, English as a second language, school public relations)—all have their arms folded when it comes to their pieces of the educational pie. Every special interest group is territorial.

There are legitimate reasons why these groups are needed. However, we need to remember that we are in the business of meeting the needs of all students in the educational system. We need to replace animosity with reciprocity. Maciejewski conveys that this sentiment is echoed by many in leadership positions within teacher unions, quoting Gerry Collins, president of the Arlington Education Association:

> Hostility doesn't get you anywhere...Conflict and confrontation are good for showing feathers, but really if the objectives are to improve instruction and to make working conditions and the working environment more positive for all employees, it's important to understand the other person's perspective (Maciejewski, 2007, p. 36).

As groups promote various agendas within the educational arena, we must know that the most important agenda is doing what's best for students. We must comprehend the significance of working together for solutions. We must realize our common ground, and we must understand that competition for students is not some fantasy on the silver screen.

Indicator # 4: Negative Publicity

If you were an investor, how would you feel about reading or listening to a negative story on an almost daily basis about the company in which you owned stock? One cannot pick up the newspaper or watch the national news without encountering a story that depicts a school employee or a school practice in the worst possible light. Read some of the headlines from newspapers in Kentucky about schools from March 2005 to May 2005 in the following chart.

Sample Headlines About Kentucky Schools

- Teacher Has Inappropriate Relationship with Student

- Elementary Reports Suspicious Man Near School

- School Board Violated Records Law

- Teachers Aide Arrested, Charged with Rape of Boy

- Student with Hit List May Face Charges

- Police Check Possible Rape at North Bullitt

- Teacher Off Job Accused of Inappropriate Contact

- Girl's Hair Set on Fire at School

- Racial Incident Sparks Middle School Anxiety

- Racial Slurs at Conner Lead to Charges

- Threat Calls Traced to Teen Girls

- Teacher Under Investigation

- Five CHSS Students Charged with Terroristic Threatening After Writing Hit List as a Prank

- Two Arrested for Assault on Student on NCHS Campus

- Child Left on School Bus

- Teacher Alleged Abuse Described in Court

- Student Arrested for Making Bomb Threats at High School

- Student Arrested After Fight at School

- Special Education Teacher Arrested

Multiply these headlines by what happens in school districts throughout the fifty states, and skepticism about the public school system becomes understandable. Citizens are bombarded with negative images of what happens in schools. And what percent of the general population is influenced by the media? According to Bruce Hunter, director of the legislative efforts of school administrators, approximately 75% of the public develops an awareness of educational news through newspapers and through television. Most people (82%) read about an educational issue via the local newspaper and convey their opinion that the local media is a credible source (Hunter, 2004).

This leads to a second disturbing realization: some people never bother to look past the headlines. That is not to say that negative things don't happen in education—because they do—or that schools should be in the business of "explaining away" what happens there—because they shouldn't.

John Black and Fenwick English, authors of the book, *What They Don't Tell You in Schools of Education about School Administration* maintain that "Teachers represent the general population. There are teachers who are sadists, child molesters, thieves, rapists, and murderers. Teachers suffer their share of alcoholism, drug problems, and psychiatric disorders. Talk to any personnel director of a large school system and they will tell horror stories that will knock your socks off" (Black & English, 1986, p. 175). The cautionary tale for public school educators is that the general public is constantly presented with a menu of options that shares *what public schools are doing wrong.* Unfortunately, the what's right message is generally overshadowed, and the entire profession suffers. This premise is supported by the results of a poll in which 60% of the public indicated that the news about public education is negative. According to surveys, over half of the general population believes public schools are headed in the wrong direction (Hunter, 2004). Ironically, the data would support the opposing viewpoint. Consider the following:

(1) Students work harder in school, take harder classes.

(2) Students are more likely to be good citizens.

(3) Students are graduating with more credits (26.05 in 2000 compared to 21.58 in 1982).

(4) The number of students taking advance placement exams has increased from under 200,000 in 1982 to almost 1,600,000 in 2002 (Hunter 2004).

The positive results achieved by hardworking staff, students, and involved parents are conspicuously absent in the media. Instead, one finds headlines and programs, such as John Stossel's portrayal of public education in a 2005 *20/20* segment entitled "Stupid Schools," that present a scathing review of some public schools.

The negative messages bantered about in some local media outlets pale in comparison to some of the criticisms leveled against public education from some of the faith based organizations, a segment of society that a majority of the people turn to for guidance, direction, and inspiration. While one might dismiss what is portrayed in the popular press as the exception, rather than the rule, what would be your reaction to your stock investment if someone you respected questioned the merit of the product? What would you do if you heard your minister or spiritual leader passionately share with you the following ideas?

- Public school students receive "an anti-Christ education."

- Public schools teach acceptance of homosexuality.

- It is foolish for Christians to give their children to be trained in schools run by the enemies of God.

- Some public schools are doing a good job ... but they are in a system that is officially and legally godless.

(Duin, 2004, p. 1)

Do these ideas incite you to action? If so, one should know that this was part of a 2004 resolution asking that Southern Baptists, a denomination with 16.2 million members, to boycott public schools. The proposed resolution was authored by Thomas Pinckney, a retired Air Force general and editor of the monthly *Baptist Banner* newspaper, and Bruce Shortt, a Houston lawyer.

An article by faith based writer and magazine editor, David Cloud entitled "The Southern Baptist Convention and the Public School System," discussed the rejection of the proposal by 70% of the delegates and provided a personal testimony to readers. Mr. Cloud portrayed the public school system as the "greatest single evil influence" on young children. The essay continued by stating that public school education is a curse and not a blessing (Cloud, 2004, p. 2).

Articles and publicity like this do not mention all the wonderful things teachers and schools do on a daily basis. Negative programs, articles, and commentaries feed the insecurities and apprehensions some people have about public education. They make it difficult to counter negative perceptions about public education and reinforce the need for schools to develop positive relationships with students, parents, and the community.

Has the Bottom Dropped Out of Public Education Stocks?

After considering the four indicators that the stock in public education is on a downward spiral, one needs to contemplate the worst-case scenario. Could public education as we know it cease to exist? Ignorance is not knowing the facts. Arrogance is knowing the facts and ignoring them. If we keep ignoring the facts and trends, or if we espouse an arrogance that public education is safe, then we may find that we are like two of the three little pigs who were confident in how they constructed their homes. When the "big bad wolf" comes and "huffs and puffs," we may experience the same level of destruction and devastation. Let's consider some possible scenarios.

Worst-Case Scenario #1: The Changing Profession for Teachers
(1) Public schools become torn apart by the homeschool, private school, charter school, virtual school, and voucher school movements. Teachers are employed by educational agencies that do not pay well, that have inadequate healthcare coverage, or that offer a retirement system inferior to current ones. Boards of education are replaced by church boards, and teachers lose some of their autonomy in what is taught and how it is taught, and even in their level of input in decisions relating to school policies and procedures.

Worst-Case Scenario #2: Funding for Public Education Changes
(2) While publicly supporting public schools, legislators at the national and state government levels will quietly express their disdain for public education by withholding dollars. Charter schools, private schools and homeschools become the norm, operating with the monies that used to be appropriated for public education. Tenure is a thing of the past. The only guarantee for students in the public education sector is the moral and ethical responsibility for special needs students. Therefore, it may be necessary to have federal- or state-sponsored special education schools. While this may

sound harsh, there is already evidence that schools who can choose their students, especially the for-profit schools that have been created as an alternative to public schools, that some choose not to educate the disabled. Educational Testing Service consultant, John Holloway (2002) shares findings from professional literature and states that "Researchers found that for-profit schools returned considerably more disabled students to the local public schools than did nonprofit charter schools" (p. 84).

Funding for public education might also be impacted as more individuals begin to draw fine lines and promote philosophical discussions about such differences as universal access to a quality education and the role of public education. Daniel E. Kinnaman (2007), publisher of *District Administration*, posits this dilemma while advocating the following:

Ensuring universal access to a quality education is imperative to the sustainability and progress of a free society, but it is wrong to assert that universal access to education is only achieved through government funded and government-run schools (p. 72).

What might be the results of such philosophical discussions? They could mirror promotion of political ideology that conveys Reagan-like rhetoric:

> The full power of centralized government was the very thing the Founding Fathers sought to minimize.... Outside of its legitimate functions, government does nothing as well or economically as the private sector of the economy.
>
> A sense of discontentment with the government and its ability to efficiently and effectively manage the programs within its embrace, coupled with the outcry from an increasing number of voices that we need school choice or a "fresh look at how best to ensure universal access to quality education in a free society may translate into funding changes for public education (Kinnaman, 2007, p. 72).

Worst-Case Scenario #3: A Homogenized Society

(3) A nation that has always prided itself on a "melting pot" philosophy and on celebrating the diversity of people will adopt an isolationist philosophy. Schools that arise out of a truly great philosophy, customizing schools to meet the needs of students, are in actuality promoting "racial, ethnic, and class isolation ... (and this) is not ultimately good for the nation" (Willis, 2002, p. 9). Further, "Parents and teachers who set up charter schools want to have a certain kind of customized schooling that attracts people who are like them. So you end up with the same kind of social stratification that already exists in the larger society" (Willis, 2002, p. 10). This is true not only for charter schools but in homeschool arenas, as well. In a 2002 article entitled "The Civic Perils of Homeschooling," Rob Reich cautions readers about the potential risks of educational systems that are customized to the desires of parents. "Customization threatens to insulate students from exposure to diverse ideas and people and thereby to shield them from the vibrancy of a pluralistic society" (p. 56). And so the scenario unfolds ...

Students will receive instruction using vastly different curricula, taught by individuals who possess a wide spectrum of training and skills—this despite the knowledge that the most crucial variable for student success is the quality of the teacher. One of the dilemmas to be faced is whether we will even associate with others who represent different viewpoints, opposing ideas, or whether we will adhere to a false belief of separate but equal education.

To prime your thinking regarding the feasibility of this scenario, reflect on what is happening. Is the fate of public schools mirroring that of public swimming pools? If we were to go back twenty years, conversation among kids of all ages and from all backgrounds would revolve around days of sun and fun at the local public pool. Today, there are fewer and fewer places for all groups of people to congregate and interact. More people have their own pools. More people have joined country clubs. The concept even plays out among churches. More churches are offering a variety of services to members of their congregation. Smaller churches are disappearing from the landscape because they cannot compete with larger churches. These large churches have more specialized services, span every type of support group, erect state-of-the-art family life centers, and recruit the "best" students for their programs, including athletics.

Even proponents of diversified schooling opportunities for students note the potential for inequity in educational opportunities because the "better programs" usually "favor children of people with power and influence" (Brandt, 2002, p. 15). Indeed, in one district that offered school choice, researchers found that "Whites left high-minority schools through open enrollment at a disproportionate rate—in one case, at a rate nearly double their proportion of the school population" (Howe et al., 2002, p. 22). The desire to be only with people who are just like oneself compromises citizenship and civic engagement. Even though Reich discusses this idea in relation to homeschools, one can generalize to all customized schooling efforts. Reich conveys the following:

> Because homeschooled students receive highly customized educations, designed usually to accord the preferences of parents, they are least likely in principle to be exposed to materials, ideas, and people that have not been chosen in advance; they are least likely to share common education experiences with other children; and they are most likely to have a narrow horizon of experiences, which can curtail their freedom. Although highly customized education for students may produced satisfied consumers, and even offer excellent academic training to the student, it is a loss from a civic perspective (2002, p. 59).

Where will the "common ground" ideas that define us as Americans be discussed and debated? Where will students learn about approaching ideas from multiple perspectives to come up with the best solution? Where will we learn tolerance and to value the uniqueness of the individual—or will we only value people who think and act just like us? Who will advocate for the children that represent the "have-nots" and plant seeds of possibility for children whose hopes have consistently been dismantled by the people they trusted the most?

In the article "The Price of Public School Choice," the authors researched forty-three schools in Boulder, Colorado, and found the following:

> The weight of evidence from our study, however, is not on the side of school choice proponents. Although market competition appears to be working, creating the greatest demand for the schools with the highest test scores and parent satisfaction ratings, concerns about the inequities associated with skimming (i.e., the tendency of academically strong students to move to high achieving schools), stratification, unfair competition, and unequal resources are well founded (Howe, Eisenhart, & Betebenner, 2002, p. 22).

The perils of thinking that produces a homogenized society— does this sound familiar to any history lessons during your school experiences?

Worst-Case Scenario #4: NCLB: A Plan for Public School Failure

(4) The No Child Left Behind (NCLB) legislation will eventually impact almost every public school in a negative fashion if it continues to exist in its current form. A range of researchers and writers proffer varying outcomes resulting from this national legislation. Some predict that anywhere from 80% to 99% of American public schools will eventually be forced to inform parents that their school did not reach *all* NCLB goals and is therefore designated as a "failing" school. Even if a school meets every goal except one, it still must wear the label "failing school." The matter becomes even more complicated when one realizes that each state has its

own benchmarks for success; therefore it is impossible to generalize about the standards for success from state to state.

One has to question how public schools can meet the goals of the original NCLB legislation. Having high expectations is imperative for success, but expecting special needs students to score at a level comparable with gifted students, as the original interpretation of NCLB suggests, defies common sense and is a certain recipe for disaster. Gerald Bracey's article "The Seven Deadly Absurdities of the No Child Left Behind" notes the following:

> It punishes the entire school for the failure of the few, often the very few. If a school's special education students fail to make Adequate Yearly Progress, the whole school fails…. NCLB requires schools to report test score data by various student categories. Most schools have 37 such categories (California has 46). Schools thus have 37 opportunities to fail, only one way to succeed. This is nuts (Bracey, 2004, p. 8).

It doesn't take long for proponents of public education to realize this legislation is comparable to the slow suffocation of public schools. Bracey maintains that the No Child Left Behind legislation is basically on a seek-and-destroy mission. He writes:

> It aims to increase the use of vouchers, privatization of public schools, reduce the size of the public sector, and weaken or destroy the teacher unions (two Democratic power bases). It contains enough inherent absurdities, though, that people of all political stripes should welcome a speedy revision or demise … (2004, p. 9)

Labeling public schools as failing to meet goals removes obstacles for private schools, charter schools, and homeschools, even though some of these "failing" schools are among the best schools in the country. Regardless of the future of NCLB—whether politicians tinker with the legislation or even abolish this particular federal mandate—proponents of public schools must be vigilant. Educators must have a heightened sense of awareness, realizing that something that sounds too good to be true and something with a name such as No Child Left Behind might be a wolf in sheep's clothing—and the wolf's name is school choice.

Worst-Case Scenario #5: Living the Golden Years with Fewer Benefits

(5) Educators who have retired or are nearing retirement may think they don't have to worry about what happens in public education. However, one should remember that retirement funds may not be as safe as one would hope. The New York *Times* published an article entitled "Once Safe, Public Pensions are Now Facing Cuts." This article examines the false sense of security among workers who "have enshrined the view that once a public employee has earned a pension, no one can take it away" (Walsh, 2006, p. 2). Many states have retired teachers and public employees who are either losing pay or benefits or seeing an increase in retirement age or years of experience, or maybe all three. Whether it is rising health insurance costs or a reduction in benefits or pay, public employees' retirement programs are being increasingly targeted in city and state budgets. If public education continues on a downward spiral, retirees may find that their benefits will parallel the plight of public schools.

Worst-Case Scenarios: A Discussion

The bottom line of all these worst-case scenarios is that public school teachers may find themselves working longer for much lower pay, fewer benefits, and more restrictions. Students may receive educational experiences that are greatly varied. Society may become more fragmented, and we may lose a sense of our national identify because we only value people who are just like us in their thoughts, beliefs, and actions. Will our knowledge and discussion concerning public education become like a page in a history book—something we read about alongside the horse and buggy, telegraphs, and the Pony Express? If the worst-case scenarios are realized, unfortunately the answer will be in the affirmative. Everyone will be surprised and say, "I can't believe it happened. I never saw it coming." Remember the comments from employees of Montgomery Ward?

As schools contemplate their efforts and rethink how we "do public education," we must look how we move beyond worst-case scenarios to improved scenarios. We can no longer be content with isolated examples of quality customer service or the "best" teachers, who seem to intuitively develop positive relationships with students and their families. Effective practices must permeate every public school and every classroom. Improving—and in some cases reinventing—public schools is predicated on courageous and inspired leadership: leadership that is committed to a set of internal principles, committed to the best interest of all students, committed to owning up to our problems, and committed to the work and communication that is required to achieve excellence for all students.

A leader is supposed to be a dealer in hope. As alluded to previously, Jim Collins identified that one of the major differences between good organizations and great organizations is that great ones confront the brutal facts. At the same time, great organizations retain a sense of faith that things will have a positive outcome. Therefore, as we look at the "brutal facts" concerning the status of public education, we need to offer a best-case scenario. There is hope, but change is required. Where does one begin? The answer is focusing on students and their needs, which unfortunately can sometimes extend beyond education and include all aspects of a student's life, even the most basic of needs. This change encompasses four major dimensions.

(1) Emphasize strong leadership.

The best-case scenario can never occur in the absence of leadership. On the best scenario game board, everyone must begin in the space labeled "Strong Leadership." This is a type of leadership that defies typical descriptions. It requires someone who can embody textbook descriptions and personify the very essence of leadership. Educational leadership of this nature means abandoning personal agendas while adopting collaborative teamwork. It is pursuit of a greater good that builds coalitions that work together in the best interests of all students. The ability to mobilize forces will communicate a clear vision and a common mission. Educational leadership is the ability to leverage legislation based not on what is politically expedient but what is morally responsible. It is a coming together, a working together, a relentless pursuit that goes beyond euphemisms and platitudes. It is the bringing together of various factions, organizations, and interest groups for a common good.

An example of this on a relatively small scale is a phenomenon that occurred during the 2004 Kentucky legislative session, when teacher unions, school board organizations, retired teachers, and others identified a common platform related to healthcare issues for public employees. To pay for increasing healthcare costs, teaching positions were slated to be cut, increasing the class size in most school districts, which would have impacted instruction in a negative manner. Based on the efforts of these groups, money was diverted from other sources in order to avert a crisis in most school districts. This included the elimination of teacher reward money for good test scores. Fragmented efforts and agendas would not have produced this same outcome. Maintaining manageable classroom size, saving teaching positions, and addressing budget issues translated into more appropriate educational experiences for students.

A second example of union members working in tandem with school administrators occurred in Kenton County, Kentucky. Teacher union leadership worked collaboratively with district and school personnel in crafting a "Quality Instruction Rubric" based on the work of Charlotte Danielson's *Enhancing Professional Practice: A Framework for Teaching*. This rubric enables individual teachers to improve the quality of instruction in their classroom by reflecting on their individual growth as a teacher in five domains. Comparable programs using peer review teacher evaluation teams and peer assistance teams have been utilized in other locales. These are examples of what Susan Moore Johnson et al. refer to as a "new unionism," which is a "call for unions and districts to work together to foster professionalism, create pleasant working conditions, make teachers feel valued, and involve teachers is governance and decision-making—all of which they posit will promote student achievement" (Hess & West, 2005 p. 38).

(2) Reduce emphasis on adult needs.

The best case scenario also begins with everyone being an advocate for students and for public education, not being benign observers and pacifiers of a process that needs fixing. Paraphrasing the character portraying the President in the film, *Independence Day*, "We can't be consumed by petty differences...we will be united in our common interests...; we should not go quietly into the night." We must come together to become advocates for students. The cause is worthy enough for all employee groups to put students first in the quest for excellence. The issues confronting schools require the creativity, leadership, and skills of everyone involved in the process. It is exciting to speculate about what might happen if these groups unite their efforts and make decisions with students as the focal point of the process. We may one day realize that *without* this collective effort, public schools, like Montgomery Ward, will quietly fade into the background. If we continue to put adult needs before student needs, our very existence may be in jeopardy!

(3) Recognize that enlightened self-interest makes sense

Ideally, educational organizations and personnel will admit when we are in error. We will change policies that promote or protect mediocrity. We will offer assistance to those within the profession who are struggling. However, we will not continually sacrifice a classroom of students year after year just so those who are not pulling their weight can have job security. We must always err on the side of students.

(4) Emphasize building personal connections with students as the
cornerstone of achieving positive learning and achievement outcomes.

Finally, we must acknowledge what is truly important in schools. We must resist the temptation to judge schools by a single indicator. Student achievement and accountability are integral to what schools are all about. However, an all-or-none accountability mentality seems to be the current standard, and everyone is losing sight of what is at the center of what we do. Caring and connecting with students must be the cornerstone of everything that is done in education; it is an integral aspect in the quest for more relevance and rigor in curriculum and instruction. Have we selected accountability over individuality? Teachers and schools have become mandated to the point that they are almost numb, resulting in a loss of the human aspect of education; everyone is functioning in a choreographed, robotic dance. We see children and students as people we "do something to," and we don't even know who they are and what they like. Teachers work hard to try to give parents, the legislators, and the community what is important. Often this is viewed as more accountability evidenced by improved test scores. However, test scores should be secondary to making connections with students. Students want to know the following:

- Someone cares about me.

- Someone knows what I like and what I am good at doing.

- Someone believes in me, even when I am unsure about myself, and will work with me to make me the best I can be.

Parents want to know there is someone at school who cares about their children—someone who sees possibilities, someone who reassures in the face of doubt, someone who will be an advocate and hold high expectations for their children. Legislators want to know the fallout of any political decisions. It sounds soft to have a "touchy-feely" goal of connecting with students. It sounds better to say that schools need to have high standards of accountability. We believe they do, but not at the expense of the students. Making high expectations and connecting with students the cornerstone of schools' efforts will result in increased student achievement and decreased dropout rates.

Best-case scenarios require us to put on a different pair of glasses in order to view something familiar to us in a new way. This requires some discomfort, some reflection, and some realigning. It necessitates that one use the "what if," "why not," and "how do we" lenses, instead of the rose-colored glasses that we usually insist on wearing.

A Five Step Process—Let's Make Our Stock More Valuable

Those within our immediate learning community have a saying that identifying a problem without offering possible solutions is just whining. While there are many avenues to counteract some of the things occurring in public education, one avenue is through a series of five steps:

- Educate

- Create

- Collaborate

- Advocate

- Navigate

1) Educate

We cannot systematically address an issue if everyone doesn't have the facts about it. The first step in overcoming obstacles in the future of public education is to have informed publics—internal and external. Jim Collins asserts that good decisions cannot be made without acknowledging the truths and facts about our organization. Heifetz and Linsky (2002) state, "People are willing to make sacrifices if they see the reason why" (p. 94). Most change literature discusses the importance of addressing the question, "What's in it for me?" If we can educate and share the message that not only is public education at risk, but also the livelihood of those who've committed years of training and dedication to making a difference in the lives of students, maybe people will see the need to enter into a dialogue, and look critically at the changes that need to be made.

2) Create

We must embrace a different paradigm concerning educational leadership. Schools must develop leadership skills in all school employees. Leadership teams with a proactive, rather than reactive, approach must help create viable solutions to the problems that plague the profession. These problems must be viewed as opportunities for leadership to create a different way of doing business in education.

3) Collaborate

Key to any successful endeavor is the ability to bring the various stakeholders into the discussion. Traditionally, education has been viewed as an institution that allows individuals to work in isolation. Not only have individuals operated in isolation, but special interest groups within the profession have done the same. Organizations must rid themselves of artificial boundaries and unite to collaborate with legislators, outlining a plan that enables public education not only to survive, but to thrive.

4) Advocate

Educators must utilize this term as a noun and as a verb. We must be an advocate for children while simultaneously advocating on behalf of public education and in the best interests of all students. Caring for students cannot be left to chance. If necessary, we must mandate caring. Someone in the public school setting must feel the pangs of failure if our students fail to achieve or fail to graduate.

5) Navigate

Schools must navigate a new and uncharted course. This uncharted course requires that everyone board the ship and, instead of sailing in a familiar direction, choose a route never taken. This requires facing our fears, working as a team, and doing what we know is the right thing to do. Blankstein discusses courageous leadership in the book *Failure is Not an Option* and shares a quote by Block, who challenges each of us in schools. He writes:

> This culture, and we as members of it, have yielded too easily to what is doable and practical… We have sacrificed the pursuit of what is in our hearts. We find ourselves giving in to doubts and settling for what we know how to do, or can learn to do, instead of pursuing what matters most to us and living with the adventure and anxiety that this requires (Blankstein, 2004, p. 29).

The adventure and anxiety we must navigate is changing the culture of the school, and one of the most important tools in this navigation is putting students first by incorporating customer service practices and intentionally making connections with students in our schools and school districts.

Change does not occur through random acts of goodness. The actions taken to address the dropping stock in public education must be intentional, focused, and systematic. We must search within our hearts and act on what we know is right. Practices must be monitored and evaluated. The changes that are needed are ones that will require courage and persistence, resources and support, as well as selflessness, wisdom, and common sense. It will take a change in belief systems and a commitment to remain on a difficult course. When students are the reason we make the decisions we do, when we institute customer service practices and change the cultures of our school, the stock of public education will soar.

Chapter Two:

Leading the Charge

Wake up to the new enemy. Embrace it, for it will transform our lives and the way we work more profoundly than we can imagine, and nothing is going to stop it.

(John Huey, Fortune, 6/27/94)

Educators have been placidly going about the way they do business for decades, reacting and responding to the latest reform, legislation, trend, or national report. In the process, an enemy has been created—and that enemy is complacency about the way we respond to students and their parents: our customers. The intent has never been to ignore the customers, but because of a bulging rolodex of expectations requiring schools and teachers to do more with less, everyone gets caught up in the task at hand. We have lost sight of the responsibility we have for our customers, for initiating and sustaining positive connections between the school and the home. As we embrace our enemy, one of the ways of transforming lives and the way we work is through changing the school culture and creating a customer-friendly environment.

Leaders do not hide cowardly from obstacles and challenges. Leaders confront reality, embracing challenges as opportunities. Transforming lives is what public education should be about. Transformations do not occur through chance or happenstance, or without the influence of someone to provide a direction and help us navigate a course for change. Instituting comprehensive customer service practices originates with leadership.

Nothing can happen in the absence of leadership. Nothing

can happen with one or two teachers championing a cause. Something can happen by teams of committed people working together to plan, implement, monitor, and evaluate a systematic process whereby students know that everything said and done in a school is in their best interest. Something very special can happen when students know that the adults in their school will partner with their parents. Something very special can happen when the adults in students' lives, especially teachers and school staff, assume an active role and have a personal, vested interest in the students' academic, social, and emotional well-being.

Making connections with students and creating a caring community within the educational setting requires a cogent, well-orchestrated initiative. Often, the simplicity of an idea is appealing, but the idea is eventually abandoned because the "how" part of it becomes complex to manage. While one can applaud the efforts of those pockets of professionals who intuitively and routinely make connections with students, that same type of effort needs to be applied on a wide scale basis. Initiatives come and go. It will take leadership to ensure that making a connection with students is the most important initiative in the district.

We are not so naïve as to believe this can be accomplished easily, quickly, and without resistance. Leadership is critical to a positive outcome, and that leadership must occur on several different fronts. The journey in our district began with questions posed during district-level staff meetings about what was most important in our schools. Did we know the students who were failing or dropping out of school? Why were students failing? How had we interacted with these individuals? How did we truly feel when a student gave up on himself and the school? How did we truly treat the customers? Did we own the problems? How did our actions relate to the basic mission of our district: that we believe in *all* students reaching their potential and that this must be accomplished with a partnership between the school and the community? How were we truly promoting this partnership?

Ideas and beliefs were debated. Members of the district leadership team began to learn about customer service and to observe how we interacted with our customers. School-level administrative teams were included in the same discussions and then worked to develop components and ideas at the yearly retreat and within classified (non-certified staff members such as secretaries, instructional assistants, custodians, cooks, and bus drivers) and certified (teaching staff) advisory committees. Strong leadership was integral and was shared by school board members, administrators, teachers, and by classified staff members.

Guess Who's Coming to Dinner

On one front, strong leadership is vital in bringing all the special interest groups together, making compromises, and agreeing on nonnegotiable expectations, procedures, and policies within the public education arena. Public education has been bullied, beat up, and even used as the doormat for what ails society, and some of our own family members are responsible for this. The leader must issue invitations for everyone to come to the table. Even though some of the members of the family aren't talking, or even if disagreements have escalated to the feuding stage, the leader must bring everybody to the table, facilitate a dialogue, ask tough questions, and listen intently to the ideas and concerns of all the family members. The leader's commitment to the task is evidenced by the fact that he or she refuses to believe it can't be done and keeps everyone at the table until there is agreement. Caring and making connections with students will guide everything that is done in schools. At this dinner party, the leader assumes the role of perfect host.

On a second front, everyone must be present and accounted for throughout the district. All must wear their commitment on their sleeve. It begins with the board of education articulating that customer service and making connections with all students is at the heart of everything that will be done in the district. The board holds the superintendent accountable. When the report card is issued for the district, there are high expectations with regard to how school staff interact with and treat students, parents, and guests that visit the schools. Customer service in the school may sound like an inappropriate idea, but everyone knows whether they have experienced it or not. If you don't think you have, consult the following examples of poor customer service and gauge your own experiences.

Examples of Poor Customer Service in Public Schools

* Negative people in front office

* Untrained students answering the phone

* Negative team leaders or teachers starting parent meetings

* Parents getting "gang tackled" by groups of teachers during conference (a term we use to describe more than one teacher conferencing with a parent)

* Staff members mistreating students

* Teachers not excited about receiving a new student in their class

* Custodial staff not treating customers in a positive manner

* Staff not responding to parent concern/call within twenty-four hours

* Staff not making positive contact with parents before calling about problems

* No one in school taking ownership for problems or for students

* Staff not placing customer concerns over employee concerns (placing teacher interests above student interests)

* Cluttered offices

* Restrooms in poor condition

* School dirty on inside and outside

* Little, if any, positive contact between parents and school throughout students' school experience

* Lapse of confidentiality (talking negatively about a student, school, or colleague with members of the community)

* Phone ringing continuously before being answered or caller must proceed through an automated phone system

* Leadership ignoring or failing to stop bad customer service practices by staff

Parents may not always share the positive experiences they have with the school system, but be assured that negative ones, such as the examples of poor customer service practices above, will be discussed in the public.

Everyone has viewed organizational charts with lines and arrows depicting the chain of command and who reports to whom. This same philosophy must be applied to implementing a district-wide initiative. The expectations will be clear, and there will be high levels of accountability for administrators, teachers, instructional assistants, school councils, secretaries, school nurses, custodians, maintenance workers, bus drivers, and food services workers. Mission statements that value quality for students and for parents (such as: "Making decisions and working in the best interests of all students") are only empty words unless every employee adopts them in daily practice. Customer service practices must permeate every sector within the school. When someone is treated incorrectly, the action should be confronted by the leadership. We want to foster the following beliefs:

• No one can compete with our school system.

• Students and their families will partner with excellent, caring staff who know each student on a personal level and work to ensure each child's success.

• You and your child are why we are here.

- We will treat you and your child the way we would like our own children treated.

- We will have high expectations for all students and offer no excuses for poor performance.

Follow in My Steps

Leadership is a show-and-tell lesson. When a leader expresses genuine concern for the well-being of the staff and students, observers—even skeptical ones—can see that the leader lives his or her beliefs. Do you remember how special show-and-tell time was when you first started school? The idea that someone cared about what was important to you made you feel valued and special. This someone allowed you to talk about what was important and why it was important to you. Remember the feeling? Leaders who listen to their colleagues, leaders who know what's important to the people who work with them, leaders who express empathy during life's difficult moments are modeling the same type of behavior students should experience from school staff.

On a professional level, leaders help develop other leaders. John Maxwell, who writes and speaks extensively about leadership, shares that the highest form of leadership is helping other people grow. The goal of leadership is to produce more leaders, not more followers. Just as great coaches develop the skills of their players and rely on the leadership of certain members of the team, school leaders need to develop the skills of the players on their team.

Why Me?

Customer service embodies all dimensions of the school organization. The first and last person to talk to the majority of students is the bus driver. The person who is most observant about hunger in a child's eye may be the food service worker. The quickest way for someone to form an opinion about the school facilities is to visit the restrooms. The person who often makes a close connection with and even encourages some students to read is the custodian.

The job of schooling is too immense to be accomplished by one person. We have modified a popular phrase and assert that it takes all the people within the school village to support, nurture, and help all children be their best. However, it takes leadership to help communicate the need, the importance, and the progress. It takes leadership to get school staff to help create the plan. It takes leadership to ensure that everyone is held accountable. It takes leadership to model and develop a culture of caring. It takes leadership to celebrate, recognize, and acknowledge sometimes even "baby steps" toward the ultimate goals. It takes leadership to empower people to find creative ways to connect to students.

Whose job is it to make sure that:

___the secretary answers the phone with a smile in her voice?

___visitors are taken to a destination, instead of pointed toward one?

___the custodian treats people who rent school facilities with respect?

___bus drivers greet each student every morning and every afternoon and use the student's name?

___teachers make phone calls to students' homes to share positive news?

___counselors and teachers provide all students with access to scholarship information and opportunities?

___students and their parents get a phone call home by a teacher after a student misses two or three consecutive days to check and let them know that they are missed?

___the custodial staff maintains schools and grounds to the same standard as Disney World?

___students and teachers are trained to make sure every new child moving into the school feels welcomed and wanted?

And the Answer is ...

It is the job of the leader to advocate for all students and to train all personnel in quality customer service, thus developing more leaders throughout the district.

Leaders must be aware of best practices in an array of areas, but they also need to know and understand what doesn't work. Schools are notorious for sending home newsletters and then lamenting the lack of parental involvement. We are not saying that this practice or the development of publications is not a good idea. However, one must know where schools should invest most of their time, energy, and resources in order to get the best returns on their investment. It is with these ideas in mind that we created a "what doesn't work" list, only as it applies to making a connection with students and their families. It has been our experience that some people think sending an invitation by the student to the parent is a good way to develop a relationship with the home. Often the invitation from the school fails to make it to the intended destination when the student is the courier. Secondly, an invitation to the masses is impersonal. This type of faulty assumption leads to a disappointing outcome.

What Doesn't Work:

- Newsletters
- Calendars
- Brochures
- Annual reports
- Radio interviews
- Newspaper advertisements
- A public relations person who is the "lone ranger"
- Handbook

What does work and offers the greatest return on one's investment is training all staff members to be public relations agents.

Leaders spend time reading, listening, and networking with others to continually learn. Educational leaders need to borrow from other professions and ascertain what practices are working and see how those practices could be applied to education. Customer service is not just an idea that applies to businesses. It is the initial step in creating a more positive image of the school within the community, and it also provides opportunities for addressing school culture and for making positive connections.

Experience is generally a very effective teacher, especially when it comes to how we like to be treated. Part of the research on implementing good customer service practices in our district was reading, interviewing managers, and reflecting on what made us think that a person or business was offering wonderful customer service. Discussions ensued about the practices that might work in education and what tools and training our staff needed in order to understand that everyone in our district is in charge of public relations and making positive connections.

Laying the groundwork for a new initiative is paramount for success. In the beginning phase of any new project or idea, it is good to be conscious of the question that many may think but never express: Why should I care? In our situation, administrative teams appealed to the teaching staff to contemplate the moral imperative we have as educators and what we would desire for our own children. This was coupled with an awareness of the importance of relationships, with storytelling from teachers who had been successful in connecting with students, and with the idea that if we want students to succeed, we must examine our assumptions that "they don't care." It began simply with commitments to beliefs and ideas and a goal of being the best school district we could be. An attempt was made to answer this question as we sought to educate, collaborate, create, advocate, and navigate for change or a shift in emphasis.

Responding to the question "Why should we care?" is crucial when implementing a district initiative on customer service. The following overview, a compilation of quotes, statistics, and facts, (some of which have been cited in Chapter 1), may be helpful to leaders as they work with staff to create a rationale for changing the way we do business in our schools. The insight comes when these ideas are used as a catalyst for discussion, and a group considers the implications for idea in their own unique situation.

Why Should We Care?

General Quotes and Statistics on Customer Service

- The Harvard School of Business discovered that 68% of customers will leave a place of business based on the indifferent attitude of a *single* employee. (Klein, 2007, p. 1)

- The average unhappy customer tells twenty-seven people about her bad experience, and with the use of Internet, that number can increase to thousands, if not millions, at the click of a button. (Sykes, 2005, p.1)

- For every customer who bothers to complain to the average business, there are twenty-six others who remain silent. (Willingham, 1992, p. 143)

- A corporation may spread itself over an entire world, may employ a thousand men, but the average person will form his judgment of it through contact with *one* individual. If this individual is rude or inefficient, it will take a lot of kindness and effectiveness to overcome that one bad impression.
(http://www.brotherblotz.com/images/motto.jpg)

- We'll spend up to 10% more for the same product with better service. (Joy, 2006, p. 1)

- If the service is really poor, 91% of retail customers won't go back to a store. (Leland & Bailey, 1999, p. 21)

- If you make an effort to remedy customers' complaints, 82% to 95% will stay with you. (Willingham, 1992)

- It costs about five times as much to attract a new customer as it costs to keep an old one. (Willingham, 1992)

Education-Related Quotes and Statistics

- Many schools have taken their customers for granted, and those customers have finally figured that out. (Jacqueline Price)

- More than 70% of parents rely on personal observations and conversations to gather information about their schools. (National School Public Relations Association)

- There has been a 29% growth in homeschools over the past five years (1.1 million students were homeschooled in 2003). (Feller, 2004, p. A11)

- Students in homeschools are scoring 15 to 30 percentile points above their public school counterparts on standardized achievement tests. (Ray, 2002, p. 50–54)

- A 2004 resolution was presented to the Southern Baptist Convention asking the membership (approximately 16.2 million) to boycott public schools. (Cloud, 2004, p. 2)

- Over 50% of people feel public education is headed in the wrong direction. (Hunter, 2005, p.12)

- Public school teachers are twice as likely to send their own children to private schools as compared to the general population. (Brondos, 2004, p. 1–2)

- Private school enrollment tripled the growth rate of public schools (6.7% versus 2.3%) from 1999 to 2003. (Feller, 2004, p. A11)

- 49% of senators and 40% of representatives have chosen private schools for one or more of their own children. (Clowes, 2000, p. 1)

- What I see is, the people running [the public schools] don't have any sense of urgency.... It's too late for you to say, "Trust me. Give me time." If my children are already in school, I don't have the time to give you. (Caire, 2002, p. 38)

The job of the leader is to ask open-ended questions and then to listen to responses. Create a dialogue with questions such as the following:

- If a parent shared this comment in our district (school), how would we respond?

- How much time would lapse between a complaint and response?

- How would the statistics on customer service look differently in our school district if we changed our practices?

- What messages are we sending to our customers by our words, our procedures, our actions, and the way we interact with the general public?

- Do we have employees who make parents or visitors to the school feel they are an imposition? How are we responding to that employee behavior? Why?

- Why are students leaving our schools to attend private schools or to be homeschooled?

- How do students in our district know we care about them?

- What are some examples of good and poor customer service in our school district?

Perhaps one of the best questions is one we term the Golden Rule question:

How would we want to be treated as a parent in this school, and how would we like our own children treated? Why? One can generalize that what would be wonderful for our own children would probably be good for all children.

School leaders need to assess their own situation and create questions that will stimulate productive conversations. Regardless, the leader must listen intently, and the atmosphere must be conducive to individuals being able to state, "I disagree with that, and this is why" in a professional manner. Poet Robert Frost probably provided one of the best conditions for listening when he penned the phrase, "Education is the ability to listen to almost anything without losing your temper or your confidence."

Frost's advice is especially compelling as one thinks about the arguments or issues that might arise when one suggests that school staff intentionally develop relationships and make connections with students—and that home visits should be an expectation. Leaders should be prepared to hear a list of excuses. One of the biggest mistakes that new leaders often make is believing that the staff will embrace a new idea because it is the right thing to do and will have a positive outcome. Resistance to change should never be underestimated. Although it is rooted in fear, resistance is usually couched in words or reactions designed to hide that fear. Prepare yourself by consulting the following list.

Why It Won't Work....

1. There's not enough time.

2. It's too dangerous.

3. Union representatives insist, "You can't make me. It's not part of my contract."

4. Parents don't want us to visit their homes, and the kids don't care.

5. That's more of an "elementary" thing.

6. We've already tried advisor-and-advisee programs. It won't work.

7. I teach content. Our school has high stakes accountability. Relationships aren't as important as teaching students content, self-reliance, and being able to score at high levels on state assessments.

8. I wouldn't know what to say.

9. The only students who might benefit would be the at-risk ones.

10. We cannot take on any more responsibility—that should be happening in the home.

11. Relationships—that's the guidance department's job.

As school leaders reflect on the race ahead, the following chart depicting the "C's" of customer service may provide some good reminders about engaging in the making connections process. Leadership can originate from various places within the organization, but it must be focused on the goals, on the process, and on continually building capacity among various staff members and celebrating the resulting successes. As we reflect on efforts toward building relationships with our customers, the following "C's" of leadership behaviors support the process.

	Behaviors:
Culture	• Build a culture of shared values, events, and rituals. • Develop a mission everyone can recite and live. • Intentionally assign staff to areas of strength, not areas of desire.

Champion	• Make decisions with *all* students in mind. • Be an advocate for doing what's best for students. • Share the positive things happening in your school.
Connect	• Connect with people (87% of volunteers do so because someone asked them to volunteer). • Model caring and support for staff. • Get to know your staff.
Challenge	• Ask questions about why we do what we do. • Ascertain what's working, what's not working, and why. • Challenge all staff to protect each other's dignity and the dignity of the learner and parent. • Confront issues, especially mistreatment of students.
Communicate	• Develop relationships and trust. They come before communication. • Ask questions and listen actively. • Know that public relations go from inside to outside (90% of public relations resources should be spent on internal communications). • Realize that there is a rank order in which people prefer to receive information: (1) direct supervisor; (2) small group; (3) large group; (4) senior management; and (5) internal newsletter (or e-mail). • Overcommunicate when the trust level is low. • Know that face-to-face communication is preferable to written communication.

Collaborate	• Develop a good relationship with media to get the message out to others. • Get staff members to work with partners or in teams to accomplish goals. • Structure the work of teams so they work interdependently.
Choice	• Involve all staff and all school areas with the initiative. • Understand that people get involved with decisions they help make; people support what they create. • Know that you will never have 100% buy-in; base decisions on the best performers.
Change	• Begin by placing data in front of people. • Answer the question, "What's in it for me?" • Promise problems. • Pilot change initiatives. • Spotlight individuals making the change.
Collect	• Collect reliable feedback. • Monitor what's happening. Have status checks. • Collect and share stories.
Celebrate	• Share successes. • Recognize those doing a good job or even giving more effort.
Commit	• Focus on continuous improvement. • Allocate time, resources, and training for all staff (certified and classified) to ensure success. • Decide on next steps after evaluating status of initiative.

As leaders search for ways to transform what schools do by intentionally focusing on customer service and making connections with students and parents, they must clearly articulate how these actions can profoundly impact students' lives. Leaders are agents for cultural changes. Change of practices is a process all the stakeholders must understand. However, one must wave a yellow caution flag about trying to do too much too quickly. Leadership must help individuals develop a process within their school or district directed toward customer service and toward making connections initiatives. Emphasis must be placed on quality over quantity. Questions must permeate the process. Clear outcomes must be benchmarks of success.

Discussions in our district have encompassed the following:

- How do we treat our customers and why?

- What changes do we need to make to mirror the best customer-friendly practices in the business world?

- How do our students and their parents know we care about them and we want them to be successful?

- How can we utilize relationship-building as the cornerstone of developing a "no-fail" culture in our schools?

- How do we demonstrate that we have high expectations for students and believe they will be successful?

The challenge to all staff is finding ways that will enable their school district to go from a good to a great district.

One of the lessons learned in our district is that teacher and administrative training programs often extol the virtue of parental involvement, but few systematically address the importance of parental involvement or the manner in which it can be accomplished. Without question, theories and methodologies are integral aspects in educational training, but one variable is often overlooked. This variable sounds simplistic and should be common sense, but it is amazing how many schools fail to evaluate their efforts in systematically addressing relationships. The power of relationships impacts every area of our lives: politically, socially, professionally and personally. Education professionals are accustomed to conversations on high expectations, accountability, rigorous curriculum, assessment, and instruction. Sadly, conversations about making intentional connections with parents and students are often absent in training experiences. However, the payoff is great. When done appropriately, the message conveyed is important and one that truly resonates with the desire of educators: *making a difference for our students*. Caring adults with high expectations have a positive impact on student achievement.

Chapter Three:

Show Me the Data

What's Your Response?

*C*offee *cups, partially filled soda cans, and legal pads adorn the top of the large conference table as principals and other district administrators engage in side conversations, awaiting the arrival of everyone for the district staff meeting. Attending the monthly meetings is a routine that is greeted with anticipation by some administrators and trepidation by others. The agenda, which the superintendent's administrative assistant e-mailed prior to the meeting, lists a status check on various initiatives, as well as a discussion on public opinion concerning schools within the district. Some of the principals contacted each other prior to the staff meeting to ascertain what information each was planning to share. After the meeting convenes, and some preliminary announcements are shared, the superintendent makes eye contact with each principal and each district administrator.*

"Do you think your school and our district are customer-friendly?" the superintendent inquires with a puzzled look on his face as he extends his open palms toward everyone around the table.

Without hesitation, and almost in unison, everyone at the table tilts their head to the side and nods affirmatively with a smile on their face. One principal volunteers, "Our schools are great. We have hard-working teachers who schedule parent–teacher conferences at least once a year, sometimes more."

There is a sigh of relief as the superintendent looks from one end of the table to the other. However, everyone's relief is premature.

The superintendent changes his expression and asks, "Is that really an accurate assessment? Is that what the public thinks, or is that what we think? What does the public really think about our schools? How do we know?"

This series of questions is met by an uncomfortable silence and a sobering realization that the responses to the questions might be a matter of perception.

Perception and Reality

"All our knowledge has its origins in our perceptions."

This statement by Leonardo da Vinci underscores the propensity we all have to analyze a situation not on data, but on our own personal experience. We are always making judgments about a place, a person, or an event. These judgments are based on our beliefs. Sometimes we feed our perceptions with other people's opinions and experiences. Miyamoto Musashi, a famous Japanese samurai and one of history's most skilled swordsmen, once stated that, "Perception is strong and sight is weak. It is important to see distant things as if they were close and to take a distanced view of close things."

As educators, we are often too close to a situation to render an objective assessment. Where do we stand in the public eye? The answer to this question is too important to rely on making assumptions we want to hear or only seeing what we want to see. We must take a distanced view of customer service. How can we see ourselves through a different lens? How do we adjust the lens so we have a clearer view of our customers' perceptions of public schools? The response to all these questions is one word: data.

Data as the Lens

Referring to his novel *This Side of Paradise*, F. Scott Fitzgerald revealed that, "To write it, it took three months; to conceive it … three minutes; to collect the data in it—all my life." Educators do not have an entire lifetime to collect data that paints an accurate picture of their school or the practices within it, but we must collect and use data if we are going to successfully compete in a contested market vying for students and funding.

Educators have become accustomed to collecting data regarding student achievement and measuring the academic success of their students and their schools. As Mike Schmoker (1999), author and consultant on school improvement and school reform advocates, "Data helps us to monitor and assess performance" (p. 35). However, application of this idea to customer service practices or to school culture may be more foreign. The gathering and sharing of data allows educators to gauge perceptions or even to gauge reality. There are a number of ways that one can begin to collect data related to customer service and to "how we do business" on a day-to-day basis. Two of the more traditional measures that offer at least a reference point for schools and/or districts are conducting school surveys and cultural audits of schools. Both of these processes provide schools with some data related to how schools operate as well as people's perception of such functions of the school as safe and orderly environment, instructional leadership, time on task, and parental involvement. Input is sought from a variety of stakeholders, including staff, parents, and students. However, these measures are sometimes plagued by an inability to get feedback from all groups, inconsistent administration of surveys, the possibility that responses to surveys are subject to personal agendas, as well as the failure to discuss the survey's validity and implications. Perhaps the greatest limitation of these traditional measures is ignoring the need to engage in self-reflective measures.

Administrators need to begin the process of assessing how responsive schools are to customers through dialogue and conversation among district administrative groups or school-level administrative teams. The process can begin with some unconventional avenues. By using a variety of lenses, schools are able to look beyond the surface and garner insights about best practices related to customer service.

Lens #1: School Caring Thermometer

Albert Einstein is probably best known for his work that gave us a greater understanding of our physical world. His words speak to the work of educators: "Strange is our situation here upon earth. Each of us comes for a short visit, not knowing why, yet sometimes seeming to a divine purpose. From that standpoint of daily life, however, there is one thing we do know: that man is here for the sake of other men." As educators, we are primarily here for the sake of our students and their families, and to help them embrace a positive image of the future. Basic to this conceptualization are a number of ideas, none more important than caring.

Relationships forge the path that leads to successful learners. Ruby Payne (2001), who is an author of books related to student achievement and poverty, as well as a chief executive officer for a company that has trained thousands of educators embraces this idea and asserts, "The key to achievement for students from poverty is creating relationships with them" (p. 142). Yet schools often view the landscape of academic achievement so intently that they fail to look at the landscape of human relations in contemplating how we "do" schools.

One of the tools that we developed for our district to begin discussions was the "School Caring Thermometer." It offers a point of departure as schools begin an introspective look at how we respond to the needs of our students, our staff, and the community. Although only five questions are posed, the response to each conveys what we value. As school leaders work together to solve problems and to establish goals related to school improvement, embracing conflict and opposing views within meetings is imperative. Capitalizing on shared thinking and asking ourselves why we utilize certain practices leads us to greater understanding of how our students and others perceive us.

School Caring Thermometer:
What Is Your School's Temperature?

1. Could a student go through twelve years of school and not receive a positive phone call to the home?

2. Could a student miss three or four days in your school or district without anyone, other than the attendance clerk, contacting the home to find how the school might help?

3. Could a parent be treated rudely by the secretary when entering the school's office?

4. What kind of plan does your school have to make sure a child new to the district or school gets off to a good start?

5. What kind of plan does your school/district have to make sure a new teacher gets off to a good start?

Lens #2: "Mirror, Mirror on the Wall …"?

Are you uncomfortable yet? Is there disagreement about the importance of "examining" our school lives? If some individuals on your staff are still skeptical about the validity of these initial conversations, perhaps sharing research on indicators of a productive school culture might prove useful. Educational research is replete with the importance of school culture and student achievement. Schools with good cultures have good relationships. In fact, Rexford Brown, in an article entitled "School Culture and Organizations: Lessons from Research and Experience," maintains the following:

> Culture is rooted in relationships. What people talk about, how they talk about it, how often they talk. How much they trust each other, share with each other or forgive each other … Organizational structures can increase or decrease the amounts of connectivity and communication among the peo-

ple in the building and between the people in the
building and the outside world.

Brown continues emphasizing the power of relationships in
schools by quoting the educational writer and researcher Michael
Fullan.

> "If moral purpose is job one, relationships are
> job two, as you can't get anywhere without them,"
> writes Michael Fullan in *Leading in a Culture of
> Change.* His chapter on the subject is entitled "Rela-
> tionships, Relationships, Relationships," to empha-
> size their importance in schools and in successful
> businesses, where they are now "the new bottom
> line" (Brown, 2004, p. 9).

If relationships are now "the new bottom line" in schools, do
our practices reflect this? How many schools are intentionally focusing on forging and developing relationships with the students?
If the job of the teacher is, as Mr. Brown writes, "To get to know the
student and draw him/her to the curriculum," how are we getting
to know the student, capitalizing on this for classroom instruction?
(Brown, 2004, p. 8). If what gets measured gets done, are we truly
planning, implementing, monitoring, evaluating, celebrating, and
providing resources dedicated to developing relationships in the
schoolhouse?

Educational institutions must be reflective organizations.
When one gazes into the mirror of school practices, it becomes
necessary to look beyond the image portrayed. The fallacy about
looking into the mirror is that the outer reflection might be a fa-
çade. Institutions, as well as individuals, have a public mask. Essential to the success of schools is ascertaining if the private mask *truly
is* the mirror image of the public one. How we treat people, how
we interact with students, staff, and the community, how we communicate high expectations, how we confront individuals who fail

to put students first—all these are indicators that enable schools to peel off the outer layers and take a good look internally.

As public schools engage in competition for students, one wonders who is truly holding the cards. Public schools want to have the winning hand, but do we? The questions outlined in "Who's Holding the Cards?" allows one to take an in-depth look at practices. As schools respond to these statements, follow up with two additional questions:

(1) To what extent do we do this?

(2) What is the evidence that we are doing this practice effectively?

Who's Holding the Cards?

Yes	No		
		1	Does every student receive a home visit before the first day of school?
		2	Can all students read at grade level or above?
		3	Do we help our parents with school supplies?
		4	Are incoming freshmen and parents assigned a teacher who will be their advocate for the next four years?
		5	Do you have a "welcoming" plan for enrolling new students, including taking care of parent issues?
		6	Are staff members excited about receiving new students in their classrooms?

		7	Do we demonstrate caring and empathy for our students, parents, and staff? Is it evident in school practices, including homework?
		8	Do we have a twenty-four-hour response rule for addressing parent/guardian inquiries?
		9	Have we analyzed all dropout records to ascertain when the problems initially occurred?
		10	If any student drops out of school, can a teacher tell you why? Does anyone display regret or concern?
		11	Do we meet with our students before they leave the public school setting (dropouts) to see if we can persuade them to stay? Can the leader save the day? Do we check back the following year to see how the student is doing?
		12	Do all teachers (K–12) attend graduation?
		13	Do we have effective transition or jumpstart programs for students?
		14	Are we honest with all our K–12 parents concerning the status and progress of their child? Do we inform early and often?
		15	Do we recruit students and set the expectation that public school employees need to send their children to public schools?
		16	Do we train and hire the best staff (certified and classified)? Do we share expectations during the interview?

		17	Do we have extensive training programs for our "front-line" employees? Do we train *all* our staff? Do we monitor, evaluate, and praise customer service with all our staff?
		18	Do we cross-train employees so that a job function can be performed by others, if needed?
		19	Do we train all coaches in customer service?
		20	Do we keep a district calendar on the Internet and ask schools to make every effort not to schedule events on the same evening?
		21	Do the school board and superintendent model excellent customer service?
		22	Does the central office provide customer service to schools? Does each school have a liaison (a designated person from central office who will work directly with that school)?
		23	Do we communicate with all stakeholders? Does the school and/or district use advisory groups, student councils, or agenda books as communication tools?
		24	Do we have quality feedback mechanisms that allow us to get an accurate picture of how others perceive our schools?
		25	Do we have a culture for growing leaders?
		26	Do all employees recover well when mistakes are made? Have they been trained?

		27	Do we "air our dirty laundry" in front of our customers (for example, disgruntled individuals, discipline, medical issues, lice)? Are these issues addressed in the front office with everyone watching?
		28	Do we confront personnel issues where individuals have responded in an unacceptable manner relating to our customers?
		29	Do our facilities look like Disney World? Are restrooms clean and well maintained?
		30	Do all students know that someone at school cares about them and wants them to be successful?
		31	Does the entire school system understand that the future of public education is under attack?
		32	Do real people answer the phone, or is the public forced to endure an automated response?

Not only do these questions enable schools to gather data through discussion and reflection about the practices within their school, they also represent thirty-two ways to win the battle for public education. As schools move from self assessment and reflection to action, school leaders must prioritize practices. Based on those results and identification of a reasonable number of activities, school leaders need to follow the process of planning, implementing, monitoring, and evaluating (PIME). It is always preferable to move at a methodical pace and do each activity well than to try to do everything at once. Emphasize quality and building a strong foundation over quantity and trying to do too much at one time.

Our district utilized these questions as a point of reference for ascertaining where we were and where we wanted to go. They allowed us to look at different aspects of the school—from facilities to communication to interacting with the public—and prioritize our efforts. The thirty-two questions are still used as a framework that allows us to revisit and reflect so that we can recalibrate our efforts.

Lens #3: Random Phone Surveys

The recipe for perpetual ignorance is: be satisfied with your opinions and content with your knowledge (Quote DB, 2007, p. 1). If schools really want to learn more about themselves, they can solicit the opinions of the customers they are serving. Relying on one's own opinions and failing to season with reflection are ingredients in the recipe for perpetual ignorance. Schools cannot afford to remain ignorant about their practices and their practices' impact on others.

One of the lenses that can be utilized effectively by schools and districts is random phone surveys. Much can be learned when school personnel call parents and ask questions to elicit concerns and opinions. The process our district uses is for the director of pupil personnel to give each person on the administrative team an information sheet or card on five students. Each district administrator and all members of the school-level administrative team make phone calls, using the questionnaire that follows. Because these data cards are distributed randomly among all the people calling, high school team members may call the parent of a student at an elementary or middle school, and the primary team might end up calling parents of a middle or high school student. The cards each person receives are truly random and include all levels and all demographics. A time period is established for making the calls, and each administrator writes responses on the customer service phone survey sheet for each call made.

Research clearly indicates that face-to-face communication is the best form for interacting with others. However, in the absence of the ability to engage in individual conferences, the telephone is a great resource. One of the benefits of "ear-to-ear" conversation is the ability to listen and ask follow-up questions. A second advantage of a phone conversation is that our school personnel have the opportunity to interject positive things about school programs, services, resources, and student achievement. As one can see from the form, every effort is made to make this an engaging and painless process for those called. Everyone is initially asked if a different time would be better for them. Questions are also limited, so that our parents do not feel as though the school is imposing on their personal time.

Merely collecting information is useless; it is what schools do with the information that adds value to the process. In our situation, principals and district administrators bring all the phone survey sheets to an administrative meeting, and the results are discussed. Results are shared, and strengths and weaknesses are identified. A number of things can happen as a result of this sharing session:

(1) If a concern is expressed by a parent, there is a follow-up to the survey phone call to make sure the situation has been resolved.

(2) Debate is encouraged to determine if there is a legitimate problem or if someone is venting, how a situation should be resolved, and what type of support could be offered.

(3) If a person is identified as providing good customer service, then that employee is contacted by an administrator, who expresses appreciation.

Finally, all responses are summarized and categorized according to the school, and copies are made and distributed at a follow-up meeting. Principals take these tallied responses and comments back to their school-level administrative teams. The compilation offers schools some qualitative data that can be used to identify recurring themes, either as strengths or weaknesses, and how this feedback might impact school improvement activities. Our experience with responses is that parents are generally very positive about what happens at school. The problems that are reported are generally related to communication issues.

The surveying process is repeated twice a year, and it is one practice that principals within our district repeatedly request that we continue. Each time the process is utilized, the district has random responses from 140–150 parents or guardians, which provide opinions and data that the schools can use.

The form used for the phone calls has been revised, and we are continually refining the process. The last question on the first phone surveys asked, "Are there any questions you have about Mason County Schools? Can we help you in any way?" Most of the time the only response elicited was a "No," or "No questions at this time." Our goal was to determine how we could improve our services; therefore, as one can see on the survey form below, we changed the question to be more open ended, requiring the respondents to think about how the school district can be more effective and more sensitive to their needs.

Mason County Schools Customer Service Phone Survey

Name of Parent/Guardian:_____

Name of Child/Children: _____

Phone #:_____

School(s):_____

Script:

I am _____, calling from Mason County Schools. We are excited about having your child attending _____ and just wanted to find out how things are going. Is this a good time, or is there a more appropriate time I could call you?

Note: At appropriate times during the phone conversation, share good things happening in our schools. See attached reference materials.

1. How was the beginning of the school year for you and your child? How could we have made things better for you?

2. Have you had any contact with your child's teachers or administrators this year? If yes: How were you treated? How was the home visit experience for you and your child?

3. Have you visited any of our schools? If yes: How were you treated?

4. If you could change one thing about Mason County Schools or make one recommendation about how Mason County Schools could be better, what would it be?

Comments	Follow-up

Sample responses from the surveys may serve as binoculars to help you see from a distant view what the process yields. The process enables us to see things we might never have had in our sight, thus altering our opinions about what we are doing and how we are doing. To help you understand what type of data is gathered, the following are examples of comments from the random phone surveys.

1. How has the beginning of the school year been for you and your child? How could we have made things better for you?

• Jumpstart Program and transition activities were helpful.

- The school is great. Parent indicated that she was ill at the beginning of the school year, which made things difficult. She also said, "Thank God I'm blessed with a wonderful bus driver (don't know name, but bus 25).

- Not real well. Child and teacher not clicking.

- Problem with another student harassing child. Nothing done last year.

2. Have you had any contact with your child's teachers or administrators this year? If yes: How were you treated?

- Everyone in the building was friendly and made child feel welcomed. Everyone we talked to was super, from principals to teachers.

- Was visited by teacher prior to start of school. This really impressed parent. She indicated she had not been visited by any other school.

3. Have you visited any of our schools? If yes: How were you treated?

- Good. No complaints at all.

- Good. Child's homeroom teacher is also reading teacher and suggested her son stay after school for extra help in reading. Child wanted to play tennis, and mother felt he needed the physical activity. Mother said she thought the teacher didn't like that very much, but that she could do extra reading with him at home.

- I have visited. I have looked to be sure that things are safe. I think they are cautious. I think they should check close and make sure who is signing kids out.

4. If you could change one thing about Mason County Schools or make one recommendation about how the schools could be better, what would it be?

- Concerned about teacher's absences, organization, and classroom management.

- Child's test scores are a concern. They are surprised they are so low. Is everyone's down or what? What do they need to do? Question about science fair—why so much time—and then science test score so low?

- Not happy with Accelerated Reader—hard to get kids to read. Push for points—hard to find books on level which interest them. Kids don't enjoy reading as much. Reading is important. Maybe they need more AR book choices. AR program isn't bad, just need to look at how it's used.

Comments:

- Parent-teacher conferences were very informative.

- Like the Internet access to grades, but please keep up better—at least once a week.

- Need milk machines along with soda machines.

- Group of teachers couldn't be any better than he has right now.

- Accelerated Reader should not affect students' grades. Reward if they read, but don't punish (grade) if they don't read.

- Jumpstart was wonderful!

- How is child being evaluated in reading?

- Disappointed with comment that child memorized reading assignment (negative vs. positive).

- Area of concern: lice.

- Bus route is sometimes off schedule.

- If it's not on the state test, student won't learn it. Almost comical, the emphasis placed on the test.

- Son got detention for being late to class. Bus was late.

- Teachers are very concerned about how students are doing. Always asking if there is any way they can help!

- Accelerated Reader stresses kids out.

The sample makes it evident that there are issues related to communication, as well as praise for staff members doing an excellent job. The data can be viewed from a variety of angles, but through an instructional lens, it is evident that the Accelerated Reader Program is an area that may need to be discussed and that the transition programs in the school system, which are known as Jumpstart, are very effective for students and their parents. Discussions among district personnel related to common concerns enable us to examine practices suggested through surveys, such as looking at how to improve the Accelerated Reader program. Parents also offered suggestions about how to improve each of these programs. Responses on other issues—such as teacher/student relationships or behavioral, academic, or social issues—require more individual attention.

Lens #4: Customer Service Feedback Cards

Have you noticed that when you eat at a restaurant, stay at a hotel, or even shop at a department store, you are often encouraged to complete a customer service feedback card or questionnaire? Businesses know one thing: the importance of offering good service to their patrons and trying to determine how they can outperform their competitors. Schools might do well to take a page out of the business book and provide parents and other community members with a quick and easy opportunity to comment about services and personnel. Our school district developed a customer service feedback card with these ideas in mind.

Asking parents, guardians, and visitors to "grade" schools is a foreign concept for many. One cannot simply develop questions on a form to be stuffed in a box—and then disregard the responses. Schools need to plan the process for developing the cards and plan the process outlining use of results. . Development of the customer feedback card must be accompanied by the following:

- Prioritizing what aspects will be included on the card.

- Insuring that responses can be generated quickly by respondents.

- Obtaining input from a variety of individuals in the development of the card.

- Training all staff on the rationale for and the use of the feedback card, including the expectation that office staff encourage visitors to complete it.

- Determining a system for placement of cards, collection, and frequency of collection.

- Insuring respondent anonymity (if desired) and determining who will have access to the cards.

The card that was developed by the staff in our school district addresses some of the priorities concerning customer service initiatives. Constructed from cardstock, the card contains three open-ended questions as well as a short questionnaire with five questions. In addition, there is a place for the respondent to check off which school or office in the district the survey pertains to.

The card is comprised of two sides. On the left side of the card are directions and three open-ended questions. The following provides the sample format and questions utilized for this section.

Customer Service Feedback Card

We ask that when you visit our schools, you grade our performance, as we try to respond to the needs of you and your child. Please pick up a card in the school office and complete it so that we may better serve you and your family.

Are you well informed about your child's progress and/or test scores? __Yes __No Comments: _____

_____

_____

_____

_____

_____

If a staff member has provided excellent customer service to you and your child, please give his/her name and describe the service provided. _____

_____

_____

_____

_____

_____

What can we do to improve our schools or to assist you and your family? _____

_____

_____

_____

_____

The right side of the card is a quick survey. Respondents are asked to agree, disagree with each question, or mark it as unobserved. The following survey format is used.

__Straub __MCMS __MCIS __MCHS __Central Office Other:	Agree	Disagree	Not Observed
I was greeted promptly and in a friendly manner.			
I was pleased with the effort made to answer my questions and/or concerns.			
My concern was addressed within a twenty-four-hour time period.			
I received positive communication about my child during the first month of school.			
The school was cleaned and well maintained.			

The school district's name and address are on the reverse side of the customer service feedback cards. Respondents are given the opportunity to mail in their card or to slide it through the slot of a locked box found at each school's office at the entrance of each building.

Feedback cards are collected on a routine basis by the associate superintendent. The names have been changed to protect anonymity, but sample comments include the following:

- I would like to thank Mr. Smith for taking the time to speak with me about John's educational future at the intermediate school. I also look to John's time at your school as a new beginning. Thank you for your positive outlook and true understanding of my frustration in meeting John's needs. I believe that my faith has been restored in the Mason County School System. Again, thank you for all your help.

- Hire better employees that don't show favoritism.

- So far, everything seems okay, except my child has been picked on and is afraid of riding the bus, even though I called the school and let them know about it!

- Ms. Jones—I was working and couldn't make it to our meeting, so she came to my work for the meeting.

This sampling of responses, positive and negative, provides valuable information about how others perceive the school and the personnel, as well as what and how we communicate with our public. The feedback cards offer the school system a great way to brag on staff members who go the extra mile and to provide great customer service to parents and guardians.

One should not expect an overwhelming number of people to take the time to evaluate the school's performance. However, the best thing about this communication tool is that people know they have the opportunity to provide feedback. School leadership teams must discuss the merits of the feedback to distinguish among an individual who is venting, an individual who is acknowledging a service they perceived as meaningful, or an individual who is pinpointing an issue or procedure that needs to be addressed. The key is always what schools do with the information they receive. We have used the customer service feedback cards to congratulate employees for their efforts with parents and students; we have also used the information to follow up on any issues identified as problematic by our customers.

Lens #5: Pledge Cards

If customer service is a focal point for the district, the commitment of all staff is necessary to reach the ultimate goal. One way a district can emphasize the importance of the customer service initiative is through the development and distribution of a pledge card for all employees. The Mason County Schools service pledge card is a credit card–sized plastic card. The content of the card was developed in collaboration with certified and classified staff. The card reads:

Mason County Schools Service Pledge

It is the responsibility of all Mason County School employees to uphold the highest standards, as set forth in the mission statement.

I PLEDGE my commitment to 100% parent and student satisfaction by:

- Knowing and fulfilling the district mission statement: *"Mason County Schools, in partnership with the home and community, will educate and assist all students in reaching their maximum potential."*

- Keeping myself informed with factual information about my school and the district.

- Addressing rumors or criticism and sharing this information with the principal or immediate supervisor, so that accurate information can be communicated.

- Addressing parents and students by name whenever possible and escorting parents, rather than pointing out directions.

- "Owning" parent concerns and complaints and following up to ensure 100% satisfaction. I will not hand off an unresolved issue.

- Answering the phone within three rings using proper telephone etiquette and with a smile in my voice.

- Always focusing on what I *"can do"* for the parent and/or student versus what I *"cannot do."*

- Taking pride in my personal appearance at all times.

- Taking pride in the cleanliness and state of repair of the school and the equipment.

- Providing 100% effort, and respecting and working closely with my fellow staff members.

I agree to follow the policies of the Mason County School System, knowing my efforts will contribute to the overall success of our school district.

The pledge card is introduced to the staff by the superintendent on the opening day of school. This is followed up by school-level administrators, who distribute the cards to all staff members and reiterate the purpose and importance of the cards. Employees are asked to carry their cards with them as a reminder of their commitment. One principal randomly offers one dollar to any employee who is the first to produce the card at a faculty meeting. The magic is not in the card itself, but in the creation of the card and the subsequent discussions. New staff members are introduced to the values and ideas related to customer service during teacher induction. The pledge card is a reminder of those values related to customer service and to expectations. The card is then used as an evaluation/discussion tool to hold individuals accountable to the ideas set forth in the pledge.

Your School's Identity

A school's identity is shaped by many factors. Every parent, even the most disengaged, wants a great school for his or her child to attend. Unfortunately for educators, what constitutes "great" varies from person to person. Great may relate to academic programs and rigor. Great may relate to programs for special needs. Great may relate to athletics and extracurricular activities. Great may relate to services offered. Great may relate to teacher quality or class size. Great might also relate to facilities. Fortunately for educators, great always relates to relationships and how individuals are treated. Many variables are beyond schools' control, but the ability to offer great customer service is not one of them. It is incumbent on schools to ask ourselves the tough questions, to reflect about what we do and how we do it, and to seek data, conventional and otherwise, that enables us to have clear responses that are based beyond the initial gut reaction. We must be able to use data to answer the question: "Are our schools customer friendly?"

Schools must be attuned to how things really are and then confront the brutal facts of their organization. In order to improve or to become great, we cannot hide behind glib sayings and assume that one or two nights a year devoted to parent-teacher conferences are going to enable us to know or respond to the needs of parents and their children. Improvement begins with honesty among the organization's leadership, through reflection and dialogue, and continues with school districts admitting the reality of the effectiveness of organizational practices. Phillip Schlecty strongly warns in the book *Creating Great Schools*:

> If the effort to save public education is to succeed, public school educators and those who support them must be prepared to be brutally honest with themselves and others. They cannot afford to whine or hide behind illusions and false claims. Happy talk and self pity may be comforting, but what is needed now are leaders who can inspire courage rather than quiet surrender and whimpering (Schlechty, 2005, p. 214).

As you think about your school and your situation, will you confront the brutal facts of how you conduct business with your customers, or are those in your school content to engage "happy talk and self pity"? How school leaders answer that question may create ripples within the field of public education. School districts that opt for courageous leadership can utilize the different tools within this chapter to begin the process of an honest appraisal of their situation.

Chapter Four:

"The" Teacher

A boy was standing by the steps on his porch when a car drove up in his driveway. The driver energetically opened the door of the car, waved at the boy, and enthusiastically greeted him with a smile, an explanation of who she was, and pleasantries that included, "I'm happy to meet you. I would like to talk to you and your parents."

The boy nodded, and while looking down and staring at the ground, he indicated that he lived with his mother. He said he would be happy to introduce this guest to her, but that would require going into the house, because she was in the bedroom. The guest reluctantly followed, only to find a pale woman lying in bed, who managed to grin and welcome the guest to her home.

As the conversation progressed, the guest learned that the boy's mother had been diagnosed with cancer and that she would be going periodically for chemotherapy treatments throughout the next few months. During this brief visit, the guest learned about the boy, his mother, and the family's interests and concerns, and she left after acknowledging to the mother and son that this would be a great year and she would do her best to help the boy and his family. The mother expressed gratitude for the visit, and there was a visible sense of relief in the faces of the mother and her son.

It had been a day of unexpected surprises. This one, brief experience changed all of them.

Who was this guest? Who was this boy and his mother? What does this story have to do with customer service and with public education? Why is the story important? Assume you are on the outside, staring through the windowpane, watching this scene unfold. Maybe it does not stir any emotion or have any significance for you, beyond being a random act of kindness, or maybe even a part of someone's job responsibility within the community. If you learned that the guest was a teacher and that the fifth-grade boy would be coming to school in two weeks, would that impact your response? What if you knew that the teacher learned that the boy's mother would be going to the hospital for chemotherapy? What if you knew that each time the boy's mom was in the hospital, the teacher would hand her cell phone to this young man so he could call and check on how his mother was doing and hear her reassurance through the phone that everything would be fine? What's your reaction? The answer is probably very different depending on your point of view. As an impartial observer, the experience might seem touching.

Assume you are on the inside, and this story is about you and your family. From that vantage point, the experience is elevated to an entirely new level. The emotions and fear that characterize this scenario are almost too painful to express. The experience is one that forever touches lives and reassures all about the value of caring and overcoming barriers and obstacles to success.

The power of a caring and effective teacher extends beyond the reach of the present and into the future. It extends beyond the four walls of the classroom and beyond the bounds of teacher's manuals and textbooks. It extends beyond the lines in a job description or in a contract. The power of a caring and effective teacher is how each child is embraced and supported for his or her individuality, how each child is held to high expectations and assured that his or her journey is not a solitary one, but a journey where someone will believe in him or her, will provide emotional and academic support, and will help each student be his or her personal best.

Maya Angelou expresses this idea eloquently:

> This is the value of the teacher, who looks at a face and says there's something behind that and I want to reach that person, I want to influence that person, I want to encourage that person, I want to

enrich, I want to call out to that person who is behind that face, behind that color, behind that language, behind that tradition, behind that culture: I believe you can do it. I know what was done for me (Hirsch, 2002, p. 2).

Organizations, institutions, churches, and schools often have mission statements that set forth a purpose for their work. Teachers who enter the educational arena with a true calling embrace mission statements that are reflective of the words of Maya Angelou. The challenge becomes: How can we live those words? What practices should characterize the work schools must do to meet the needs of our customers (parents and students)?

Who Cares? We Should!

Skeptical educators reading or hearing words like these often label as bleeding hearts those who advocate such ideas, or perhaps visualize a best practice as sitting around holding hands and singing "Kum Ba Yah." They hold that the purpose of school is to teach and not to cater to students, believing a professional aloofness prepares students for the eventuality of the "real world." Their mentality is that, once a lesson has been taught, it's up to the students to "get it." Lessons are taught, grades are given, and success is judged by whether the teacher is covering the content. Some of these individuals lament that the school cannot take on those responsibilities that are ignored by the home or the community. This conceptualization of teaching ignores the complexities intertwined with instructing, learning, and achieving. It wages war on the idea that learning is predicated on relationships. This conceptualization of teaching taunts those who are cognizant of the fragile nature of life, the circumstances that can make even the strongest vulnerable, and the dynamics of emotion, safety, and security as they relate to the brain and learning.

Some of the statistics haunting public education underscore the various dimensions of teaching and the realities confronting teachers. In 2005, The National School Public Relations Association conducted a study of high school student engagement of 904 ninth through twelfth graders. The statistics and data garnered from such sources cannot be ignored and must be used to inform school practices. Consider the following:

Sound the Alarm!

- 30% of high school students do not have a conversation with an adult; *(on any given day)*

- 48% of students feel that schools do not care about them.

- 40% to 60% of rural, urban, and suburban students become chronically disengaged from school—not counting those who've already dropped out

- 36% of students are not involved in school-sponsored extracurricular activities; 42% of general education students and 49% of career/vocational students report spending "no time in school-sponsored activities."

- 50% of high school students seldom receive prompt feedback on assignments; 53% feel comments are not meaningful or helpful.

- 53% of students care about their current school, but only 47% would choose the same school again if they could select their school.

- Only 31% feel that school rules are fair, and 50% of students believe that schools try to treat students fairly.

- 67% of students feel that school staff accept them for who they are.

- 55% of students feel safe at school.

- 72% of students rate schools as placing a major focus on athletic achievement, compared to 63% identifying academic achievement as the emphasis (Klem & Connell, 2004, p. 262; HSSSE Findings, 2006).

An interesting discrepancy in the 2005 High School Survey of Student Engagement occurred between students who reported being engaged and feeling supported and respected by teachers and those who did not. One word of caution is needed about interpreting the following tables. The category "strongly disagree" represents one subset of students, and "strongly agree" represents another subset of students, so one should avoid the urge to combine the totals. Examine the first table which contains responses for students who strongly agreed with the statement, I am supported by teachers. These students are highly engaged and see a connection between what they are learning and their future. Now examine the second table containing responses from the group of students who strongly disagreed, I am supported by teachers. School for these students is a very different experience.

Table One:

	Strongly agree I am supported by teachers
I take pride in school work	86%
What I learn at school is useful	75%
I have opportunities to ask teachers questions about work	89%
I am challenged to do my best work at school	75%
I feel safe at school	74%

Table Two:

	Strongly disagree I am supported by teachers
I take pride in school work	28%
What I learn at school is useful	19%
I have opportunities to ask teachers questions about work	22%
I am challenged to do my best work at school	18%
I feel safe at school	19%

Sixty-five percent of students who strongly disagreed that they were supported and respected by teachers were males. Differences among the groups in the survey, including the gender-related one, beg the question, Why? The High School Survey of Student Engagement, noted as one of the largest national databases on this topic, does not offer any analysis of the survey results, but it provides data about the importance of teacher-student interactions, as well as the need for an intentional focus on relationships.

Some of the faces roaming crowded hallways between classes are haunting as well; they are silently screaming for someone to notice them. It's frightening to see the number of students who walk through the schools' hallways while making little or no eye contact, with blank expressions on their faces, and with an appearance of disconnectedness that should create alarm in all those who observe them.

The implications for schools and for educators are staggering. Student achievement is rooted deeply in teacher-student relationships. In fact, Ruby Payne posits that for impoverished students, "the most significant motivator for these students is relationships" (p. 142). She includes a quote from an article entitled, "Invincible Kids" from *U.S. News and World Report* that underscores how important relationships are in the schoolhouse: "Locate a resilient kid and you will also find a caring adult—or several—who have guided him" (p. 142).

Those of us involved in education can no longer bury our heads in the sand and pretend that the school does not have a responsibility to engage all students and make them feel supported and valued at school. We can no longer leave this dimension to chance and to the efforts of some of the teachers. There must be a concerted school effort to study what students are telling us, to critically assess our practices, and to make changes that will bring all the players to the table. The research is clear that engaged students get more from school than their disengaged counterparts (Fredericks et al., 2004, p. 59–109) and that "relationships between teachers and students are an important aspect of the school experience" (HSSSE, 2005, p. 6). Teacher caring and supportive interpersonal relationships have been linked to increased student learning, greater school satisfaction, and more positive academic values and attitudes toward school (Klem & Connell, 2004, p. 262).

Unfortunately, the words, "I don't care" are not only murmured by some of the students within schools, but they are often unintentionally reinforced by school employees' attitudes and practices. These words would be almost nonexistent in schools that are attempting to develop learning communities. Robert Turner in a fact sheet on understanding poverty credits Dr. James Comer, Yale professor of child psychiatry and associate dean of Yale Medical School, with the idea that , "No significant learning occurs without a significant relationship" (Turner, 2003, p. 2). Relationship building is the common thread among the research and practices related to closing the achievement gaps that exists within schools. Yet the concept is so foreign in our schools that we almost identify it as a novel practice, especially at the middle and high school levels. Staff must be reminded that relationship building is the cornerstone of the work that is done within school.

Dr. Lorraine Monroe, principal and author of the book *Nothing's Impossible*, cited a research study involving 250 children who were successful despite a terrible home life. These students attributed their ability to surmount life's most difficult obstacles to one of three common themes.

(1) There's a way to escape. (Schools give hope.)

(2) They believe there is something better out there.

(3) Each had found "somebody for them."

Schools must embrace their role, an ever demanding and changing role in educating students. Students must know that at school there is "somebody for me"—some adult who cares enough to believe in them, to advocate on their behalf, and to hold them accountable for what they might become. This is not an easy role for schools, but it is a moral imperative, given the conditions that many of today's parents and students face. If students could talk with their educators, this is what they would say.

Student Voices: About Me …

	Know my interests and gifts.
	Have high expectations for me, and hold me accountable.
	Affirm that I am smart, and I can learn through your words and actions.
	Know what my resources are, but don't embarrass me in front of others.
	Treat everyone in the classroom with respect.
	Acknowledge that being different is something to celebrate.
	Get me involved in school activities and events.
	Listen to me and talk with me.
	Help me succeed in school, even if it means working beyond the school day.

	Give me choices and make learning relevant.
	Give me hope about the contributions I have to offer the world by asking, "What are you going to accomplish today that is great?"
	Notice when I'm having a good day and recognize me, or if I am having a bad day, reassure me.
	Create an environment that says, "It's okay to take risks or to make mistakes in this classroom."
	Come to watch me at something that is important to me (play, ballgame, recital, etc.).
	Stretch and challenge me.
	Create an atmosphere in the classroom and the school that communicates, "We will not allow anyone to fail in this school."
	Help paint a picture of what my future could be.

Teachers can also learn from students' delineation between good and poor teachers. The implications from a listing of positive characteristics in a teacher from a student perspective should speak volumes to those concerned about creating great schools and engaging classrooms. Students can articulate clearly about what effective teachers do in their classrooms and how it is conducive to a positive learning environment

Student Voices: About Teachers

Good Teachers	Ineffective Teachers:
Make sure students do their work	Complain about everything and everyone
Control the classroom	Don't care about students

Help students whenever and however students need it; they don't say, "Look it up"	Aren't interested in students learning
Explain assignments and content clearly	Sit the entire period
Vary classroom routine and use different instructional strategies	Tell students to figure it out for themselves
Take time to get to know students and their circumstances	Say negative things like "You will fail," "Shut up," "You should know that," or "You won't amount to anything"
Push or challenge students	Are always on the computer or cell phone
Work with everyone	Convey to students they just have to show up for a grade
Encourage students	Lecture all the time
Show students how they can improve by offering comments about their work	Seldom give students feedback on their work
Corbett & Wilson, 2002, p. 18; Kentucky Department of Education, 2006; Mason County Student Focus Group, 2006.	

Mason County uses information from the chart to identify areas for celebration and areas for growth. Caring is a "show-me" phenomenon for students, not a "tell-me" one. "Show me" is evidenced by knowing who students are as individuals. "Show me" is also evidenced by the presence of certain teaching behaviors. Good classrooms are places where students believe that the teacher refuses to give up on them. Schools must never lose sight of integrating effective teaching practices, as well as finding ways to show students we care about them and their future.

As teachers contemplate what classrooms built around the idea of forging relationships might look like, the ideas in the chart above are evident in research cited by Ruby Payne (2005–2006) dealing with interactions between teachers and low-achieving students. Payne identifies fifteen teacher expectations that result in student achievement gains. These ideas offer teachers the opportunity to reflect on their classroom and allow administrators to consider all classrooms within their school.

Building Relationships

Do I ... or Do We ...

1. Call on everyone in the room equitably?

2. Provide individual help?

3. Give wait time (allow student enough time to answer)?

4. Ask questions that give students clues about the answer?

5. Ask questions that require more thought?

6. Tell students if their answers are right or wrong?

7. Give specific praise?

8. Give reasons for praise?

9. Listen?

10. Accept the students' feelings?

11. Get within an arm's reach of each student each day?

12. Demonstrate courtesy to students?

13. Show personal interest and give compliments?

14. Touch students (appropriately)?

15. Desist (do not call attention to every negative behavior)?

(Payne, 2005–2006, p. 2)

Harry Wong, author of the book First Days of School, shares that students want to know seven things on the first day of school. It is interesting to note that all seven have to do with expectations and with student and teacher interactions, a major corollary to student achievement.

7 Things Students Want to Know on the First Day of School	It is …	It is not …
Am I in the right room?	• Standing at the door • Greeting students • Providing directions about expectations • Having a bell-ringer activity	• Visiting another teacher while students are entering your classroom • Being on the computer/cell phone • Forcing students to guess what to do when they enter
Where am I supposed to sit?	• Having a seating chart, names on desk • Being purposeful about seating arrangement	• Allowing first come, first served seating preference
What are the rules in this classroom?	• Having a short list • Being specific • Understanding what is acceptable and unacceptable • Teaching routines and procedures	• Having a ten to twenty item list • Stating rules negatively • Creating a "build the plane while in flight" enterprise

What will I be doing this year?	• Being specific • Providing a variety of learning activities • Including student interest and choice • Engaging, with students actively involved • Sharing why students need to learn information, how they will use it, or how it connects to prior or future knowledge	• Reading the textbook in sequential order and answering questions at the end of the chapter • Listening and taking notes only • Forcing students to be passive receptors
How will I be graded?	• Giving specific and meaningful feedback • Providing opportunities for mastery learning, • Self-assessment and student reflections • Including a variety of assessments • Providing interventions and extensions • Being fair and consistent	• Giving a surprise exam at the end of the six or nine week period only • Using only one or two grading measures

Who is this teacher as a person?	• Letting students know about you, your interests • Sharing what is important to you • Giving students an opportunity to determine similarities between you and themselves	• Allowing students to do whatever they want • Proceeding as a robot and ignoring the importance of developing a good teacher/student relationship • Exposing students to roller-coaster behavior (up one day, down the next)
Will the teacher treat me as a human being?	• Being fair and consistent • Knowing what the students' interests are • Helping students believe they can be successful even when they are struggling • Caring about what students do outside of school • Helping students learn better ways to handle situations • Valuing students' ideas and input	• Yelling at or embarrassing students • Talking about students in a negative way to other students or people • Putting students down in class • Not keeping a score card or running list about everything students do wrong

Schools that succeed in motivating alienated students "inspire students with strong feelings of membership, engagement, and commitment" (Sagor, 2002, p. 34). The ways schools structure educational experiences to address these components differ, but central to each method is the students' basic understanding that they belong. The ideas of membership, engagement, and commitment are important to all learners. Schools must be deliberate about their actions; actions must progress beyond writing a policy. The Board on Children, Youth, and Families has noted that "Increasing motivation and engagement is unlikely to be accomplished by simple policy prescriptions such as raising standards, promoting school accountability, or increasing school funding—although these might be helpful in the right set of circumstances" (National Academies Press, 2003, p. 14). The educational enterprise is a one-on-one endeavor, and education professionals must be astute in understanding how to engage learners.

In an article entitled, "Invitations to Learn," Carol Ann Tomlinson identifies similar ideas, but she offers readers a different framework to insure that teachers are meeting the five student needs that will engage students in the learning process. The following chart provides an overview of the five needs and affirmations that must be addressed within each area. Students need to know, feel, and believe that schools and learning experiences adhere to the basic set of ideas within each of these areas of student needs.

Area:	Beliefs of Students:
Affirmation	I am accepted here just as I am.
	I am safe here—physically, emotionally, and intellectually.
	People here care about me.
	People here listen to me.
	People know how I'm doing, and it matters to them that I do well.
	People acknowledge my interests and perspectives and act upon them.

Contribution	I make a difference in this place.
	I bring unique and valuable perspectives and abilities here.
	I help other students and the entire class to succeed.
	I am connected to others through mutual work on common goals.
Purpose	I understand what we do here.
	I see significance in what we do.
	What we do reflects me and my world.
	The work we do makes a difference in the world.
	The work absorbs me.
Power	What I learn here is useful to me now.
	I make choices that contribute to my success.
	I know what quality looks like and how to create quality work here.
	Dependable support for learning exists in this classroom.
Challenge	The work here complements my ability.
	The work stretches me.
	I work hard in this classroom.
	When I work hard, I generally succeed.
	I am accountable for my own growth, and I contribute to the growth of others.
	I accomplish things here that I didn't believe were possible.

Tomlinson 2002, pp. 6–10.

The ideas contained within Tomlinson's five major needs of students are valuable reference points for teachers. In fact, teachers can utilize the works of Payne, Wong, and Tomlinson to formulate some initial understanding about developing positive teacher and student relationships and the implications for student achievement within the classroom. Secondly, teachers can utilize these charts as tools for self-reflection and planning regarding the instructional activities needed in the classroom and then look at systematic ways to make these behaviors evident in class interactions, expectations, and activities. As schools reflect about how they do business, they must evaluate their supports systems and efforts and can utilize some of the ideas contained within the book, *Engaging Schools: Fostering High School Students' Motivation to Learn* (National Research Council, 2003). The following list adapted from this source is a starting point for schools as we ask ourselves to what degree do we have the following?

❑ A challenging curriculum with opportunities for students to incorporate areas of interest and one that enables them to understand and apply what they know

❑ Knowledgeable, skilled, and caring teachers who truly know their students

❑ A school culture that is focused on students and on learning

❑ A learning community that provides support and a sense of belonging, with opportunities to interact with academically engaged peers

❑ Strong ties linking the school with students' families and communities

❑ Interventions that convey to students that "We refuse to let you fail"

❑ An organizational structure and services that involve all students and address nonacademic needs

❑   Opportunities to learn the value of schoolwork for future
    educational and career prospects

One must look at these like a district attorney and ask what
evidence exists to find schools guilty beyond a reasonable doubt of
all these practices.

Beyond Being Overwhelmed: A Starting Point

Parents and students want a caring teacher. What does caring
mean? Judith Deiro (2003) maintains that "Caring is not just a way
of acting; it's a way of thinking." According to Deiro, caring doesn't
have to mean being all "nicie-nice. Being permissive, sweet, warm,
or gentle is not the prerequisite of caring. Caring teachers can be
stern and strict ... But they must be respectful to be perceived as
caring" (p. 60, 62). Caring encompasses knowing your students.
That does not mean administering an interest survey the first day
and then filing it away, never to be used again. It means knowing
what students like, what concerns they have, and who they are as
people. Caring means helping students be successful.

Home Visits

One of the best ways for teachers and schools to get to know
their students is through home visits. When educators, especially
middle school and high school educators, hear the words "home
visit," immediate panic sets in, and we start making excuses about
why having teachers do home visits would never work in our school
or community. Suspend judgment for a few minutes and think
about the possibilities this initiative could have in your school or
district.

Mason County School began the "Making Connections" initiative three years ago as a part of an emphasis on improving school
culture. Within contemporary education literature and among the
experts, many lament the fact that schools today lack rigor and
relevance. Mason County School leadership and teachers believe
that one cannot have rigor and relevance before having relation-

ships that focus on knowing students, on involving families, and on helping our students peer through the crystal ball of the future to visualize their future role in our community and society.

True understanding of another is based on knowing that individual. Knowing students cannot really occur without having the opportunity to interact with students and their family in the territory where they are most comfortable: their home. Many parents find school an intimidating place with people who put students into categories and predetermine what is possible for a student or a group of students. Each of us wants to be treated with respect, wants people to look at us and see our possibilities, wants to add value to others, and wants to be recognized for our individuality and uniqueness. Ironically, the things that make us unique are also the things that bond us together as human beings. Maslow had it right when he stated that people have basic needs, that people need to feel safe and to belong—and that, before anyone could realize his or her true potential, certain needs had to be met.

"Making Connections" has enabled our students and families to feel more valued and to make our staff truly appreciate the circumstance of each child. Staff members are going the extra mile to make sure that students know there is someone at school who cares about them, not as a number, but as a person, that someone wants them to succeed.

It would be inaccurate to imply that this initiative was a result of everyone nodding their heads and saying, "Yes. I want to do this." Everyone agreed on the importance of it but expressed much trepidation. As the change process literature suggests, one must make sure to address all the issues. Some of the decisions that needed to be made included the following:

Issue	Discussion Highlights	Decision
Who do we visit?	❏ All students ❏ At-risk students ❏ PreK–5th ❏ PreK–9th ❏ High school students (who won't want home visits)	❏ All students will be visited K–12, because in some ways, all are at risk. ❏ We don't want to single out certain students so that visits are viewed as a negative. ❏ All students, K–12, look forward to visits from their teacher.
When do we visit?	❏ Throughout the school year ❏ Throughout the summer ❏ Prior to school starting	❏ We will visit the middle of July through the end of August (most teachers complete visits by the first day students come to school)
What do we do?	❏ Share expectations ❏ Outline projects for the year ❏ Provide lists: book list, supply lists ❏ Learn about student and family ❏ Document day and time visited	❏ Find out about the student. Learn about interests, gifts, likes and dislikes, and any special issues. Everything else is secondary. ❏ Document day and time visited (Some teachers make notations to use later after leaving the home.)

What process is used to schedule home visits?	❑ Drop by or show up ❑ Call and schedule a time ❑ Write a letter ❑ Offer to meet parent at a neutral location	❑ The process varies, based on teacher preference. Calling and scheduling an appointment is a middle class value; probably 60% of our students from poverty might be uncomfortable (Ruby Payne). ❑ Scheduling general times ("I'm coming during this two-week period") seems to work. ❑ Scheduling specific times at each house takes away from the spontaneity of the visit.
What are the fears and barriers related to this practice?	❑ Safety ❑ Dogs ❑ Fear of being uncomfortable or unwelcome	❑ Teachers could pair with another colleague. ❑ Schools could find another adult (guidance, administrator, family resource) to accompany any teacher. ❑ Dogs proved to be the primary issue. ❑ When teachers encounter homes with signs indicating, "Stay out," and warn of personal injury or harm, parents are contacted and visits scheduled at another site

How are administrators or administrative teams involved?	❑ Provide training utilizing teachers and other staff members who had conducted home visits ❑ Establish expectations ❑ Accompany teacher ❑ Visit students and families who are seen in office on frequent basis ❑ Monitor	❑ Provide training utilizing teachers and other staff members who had conducted home visits ❑ Establish expectations ❑ Accompany teacher ❑ Visit students and families who are seen in office on frequent basis ❑ Monitor
How should staff members dress when doing home visits?	❑ Dress casually, but neat	❑ Dress casually, but neat
What should one do upon arriving?	❑ Remain outside ❑ Ask to go inside of home ❑ Go inside if invited	❑ Visit can be on porch steps, out in yard, or, if invited, in the home (depends on the situation).

What if no one is at home?	❏ Don't worry about it ❏ Leave a note ❏ Call ❏ Call and reschedule ❏ What is a good faith effort?	❏ Leave a note. ❏ Call and reschedule. ❏ Follow the good faith guidelines.

This is not an exhaustive list, but it should provide ideas about some issues related to conducting home visits. One must listen to concerns and attempt to address them prior to having staff embark on this adventure. Each district or school must blaze its own trail and create a list of "best practices" that ensure consistency among the students and staff. The best practice list for home visits for Mason County is included; however, the secret is school personnel working collaboratively to develop the documents and processes to be used for their respective situations. Mason County staff members developed door hangers, magnetic business cards with teacher contact information for refrigerator, plastic packets of information to leave with the family, and other resources to use during their home visits. Examples of documents and guidelines follow.

Mason County Intermediate School Home Visit Log

Student:_____

Teacher: _____

Date: _____

Time: _____

___Child was home

___Child was not home

___Parent was home

___Parent was not home

Hello, I'm _____, a teacher at Mason County Intermediate School. Your child, _____, is in my homeroom, and I just wanted to stop by, introduce myself, and see if you had any questions about the new school year. We want to make sure your child has a successful experience. May I ask you a few questions?

1. What are your child's hobbies and favorite activities?

2. What are your child's academic strengths?

3. What transition concerns do you have about your child attending the intermediate school?

4. What other questions or concerns do you have about our school?

Home Visits

Suggested Materials or Information Needed:

Enrollment forms

FYI postcards

Home visit script

Class supply list

Newsletter

Brochure from individual teacher or triad

Magnets or business card

Pencils, bookmarks

City/county map

Updated rosters from STI

List of at-risk students: If possible, a member of the administrative team would like to conduct a home visit with the teacher for at-risk students.

A successful home visit is a good faith effort to develop a positive relationship with the family to insure student success:

* by establishing an open line of communication

* through face-to-face contact

* by visiting the residence of the child.

If parents are not at home, schools have developed tools such as door hangers and post cards to let parents know the teacher made an initial visit. The following post card is an example from the intermediate school. If the family was not home, teachers follow-up with a second visit at a later date.

Welcome to Mason County Intermediate School

We stopped by to visit you and your child today. Sorry we missed you! If you would like to receive any information or would like to reschedule a visit, please contact us by phone, fax, or mail.

Phone: (606) 759-2000
Fax: (606) 759-2001
Address: 720 Clarks Run Rd.
Maysville, KY 41056

DATES TO REMEMBER:

August 4th & 5th	Jumpstart for 3rd-graders	9:00–12:30
August 5th	Open House	7:00–8:30
August 6th	Back to School Fair	3:00–7:00
August 11th	First day of school	

Teachers who had been conducting home visits on their own in our district, as well as guidance counselors, proved to be a great resource in developing and implementing this initiative. These individuals provided professional development related to conducting home visits, led discussion groups, helped distinguish between myths and realities of home visits, and often volunteered to accompany those who were unsure about conducting home visits. Teachers were also asked to review the notes from the previous year prior to their own visit. Schools throughout the district have collaborated to develop a best practice list. This best practice list is reviewed annually and then utilized to train new staff members.

Home Visit Best Practice Checklist
1. Vary schedule to accommodate parents.
2. Call ahead or send out a letter with a window or a timeframe indicating when you will be conducting your home visits.
3. Prepare before visiting. Preview student success plans, prior home visit records, or Individual Learning Plan. Think about a conversation starter.
4. Wear casual attire and use casual conversation.

5. Listen and learn—remember, this is an informal visit.
 	
    ☝ Find out *common* interests between the family, the student, and yourself. (Hint: Notice the environment—Is there University of Kentucky memorabilia? Is there a garden? Did you notice any pets?)
 	
    ☝ Learn about the *student's interests and activities*.

6. Limit the number of staff members visiting a home to two people. This decreases the intimidation factor.

7. Be positive, and share good things about the school, especially programs or activities that the student might be interested in pursuing.
8. Reassure the parents you are there for their child. The goal is to work together to make sure the student is successful.
9. Discuss how and when the parent can contact you with any concerns or questions.
10. For new students, conduct a home visit within the first thirty days.

Ironically, one of the areas about which faculty expressed concern revolved around the question of "What do we say? What should we discuss during the home visits?" This probably occurred as a result of staff members being concerned about making good first impressions. The high school counseling department developed a list of prompts to encourage open communication that was used for training and to alleviate any concerns the faculty might have about conversing with parents and students during the home visit.

Talking It Over

* What do you enjoy doing? Why?

* Do you enjoy your new school (freshmen, new students)?

* If you know a family member, ask about him or her.

* What is your favorite thing about school? Least favorite? Why?

* What do you enjoy doing when you're not in school?

* What extracurricular activities are you involved in? If not, suggest involvement.

* What are your plans after you complete high school?

* Who are your best friends? What do you enjoy doing with your friends?

* What motivates you in school? In life?

* What concerns do you have about school for the upcoming year?

* What would make school better for you?

* What can I do to help you be successful?

* Have you been recognized lately for any special achievement?

One may also anticipate ways for faculty to share home visit stories. These become a rich and valued school tradition. Listening to stories similar to the one at the beginning of this chapter become part of the shared experiences of the school family and validates the reasons that the hard work and time are worth the effort. Our school district rotates its board meetings at each school, and one of the items on the monthly agenda is staff and student spotlight . The student and staff highlights often focus on home visits, with teachers recounting the significance of the visits to students, to parents, and to themselves. One cannot underestimate the power of these visits, even though there is a tendency for some people to wonder what difference they are making in our schools. In October 2006, a high school math teacher, Chy Rose, shared with the principal a story about her experiences.

Experiences from Chy

I started fresh this year, with twenty-eight new freshmen to visit. For some reason, everyone that came into the school fell into my group of alphabetized kids (Homerooom lists are generated alphabetically, using a student's last name). By the time I got down to the last three, I will admit that I wondered if I couldn't just slide on by, not bother, without anyone finding out; how glad I am that I finished up. Most of my visits had been: how do they pay for lunch, how much time between classes, and so forth.

During the first of my last three visits, I found out that the freshman girl was pregnant. She had a miscarriage in the spring, so they were watching her closely to see that things would be okay this time around. The mother had many questions.

The next child I visited is going deaf. She has two hearing aids, $5,000 each. The parents wanted all kinds of information on how to approach this. Did we offer classes for the family, and so forth.

The last student was living with her aunt. She said her mother lived down the street with a brother. She wanted to know how to get a job. Since she was only fifteen, I asked her if she was just wanting some extra spending money; but no, she needed the money to help pay for her mother's funeral expenses when she passed away. Her mother had cancer and didn't have long to live.

These last three visits made all the others worthwhile. You never know, when a child is sitting in your class, the types of problems they are dealing with on a daily basis. I was able to inform the teachers of the students about their difficulties, so they would have a better understanding of the children. The third child's mother has since passed away. The student brought in a scrapbook with pictures of her mother for me to see. Without the home visit, I do not think I would have been a person she would have been comfortable sharing her thoughts and feelings with. I have a star by her name. She has told me that she promised her mother that she would finish school. I hope to help her meet this goal.

Expect to hear resistance at the middle school and secondary levels, but don't equate resistance with an inability to do home visits or to make connections. The visits are too important to acquiesce to a few people who love their status as the squeaky wheel, always finding reasons why things won't work. One approach at the secondary level is for teachers to "take custody" of their students at the freshmen level and continue "living" with them for four years. In fact, this teacher in Mason County is the individual who will hand the students their diploma at graduation.

The high school follows the same best practice checklist as the other schools in the district, but teachers are also trained in planning and preparation procedures, which include the following:

- Calling and making a general appointment

- Taking a card to leave if no one is home

- Taking information about the start of school, clubs, the Individual Learning Plan

- Knowing the names of the parents and/or guardians

- Giving tips on how to be most successful in high school

- Leaving contact information and encouraging attendance at PTSO, parent conferences, and school events

- Varying schedule to accommodate parent schedules

- Documenting date and time of visit

- Visiting new students within the first thirty days of enrollment

The Individual Learning Plan (ILP) is a great tool to utilize during home visits; it helps teachers make connections with students. The high school counseling department recommends teachers to use the ILP to do the following:

- Assist with transition

- Provide comprehensive data regarding student success

- Help students see the relevance of learning

- Help students establish realistic career goals

- Assist in planning high school coursework

- Solicit input from parents

- Help students take responsibility for their career decisions

Making Connections Beyond Home Visits

Home visits are only one avenue the district utilizes to make connections with students. Teachers make time to individually connect with students in the classroom. The high school periodically offers an extended homeroom period to ensure there are times allocated for fostering connections between the students and their teachers. Suggestions are made by the counselors for extended homeroom periods and include some of the following expectations:

- *Talk individually with students as much as possible. Show you care!*

- *Be personable and interactive with all students.*

- *Ask questions. Let the students do the talking.*

- *Monitor discipline/attendance/grades; intervene early if problems are evident.*

- *Make students' goals and plans a central theme of conversations.*

- *Emphasize higher education and training.*

- *Encourage extracurricular involvement (membership and leadership).*

- *Model good character, and encourage respect.*

Identification of Essential Skills

All schools are incorporating a select list of "essential skills" borrowed from Ron Clark's *Essential 55*. The select list is viewed as "soft skills" that all students need to be successful. Each school's list focuses on seven or eight areas and include the following:

- Good manners/etiquette

- Communication (expressive and receptive skills)

- Working with others (social skills)

- Organizational skills

- Diversity awareness

- Conflict resolution

- Accountability for actions

- Resume writing/interview skills

- Job skills

- Literacy

These skills are to be taught, modeled, and continuously re-viewed and reinforced, beginning at the primary level. One example of this successful practice is at the middle school level. Students demonstrate their understanding of one of the essential skills in a real-life setting during a manners/etiquette unit within the practical living class for all 8th-grade students. This culminates with all students "dressing up" to visit a local restaurant for a lunch in which they demonstrate their manners. Reflecting on the experience upon returning to school is an integral component and has resulted in positive feedback from students, teachers, and the community.

Impact of Making Connections

The impact associated with home visits and making connections is evident from a variety of sources. One of the most heartwarming sources comes from students' comments. A high school teacher recounted with tears in her eyes the power of being thanked for being a "school mom" and not allowing her students to fail or get in trouble. The student had constructed a "homemade" card expressing gratitude to this teacher. Stories and comments from our teachers demonstrate the intrinsic rewards and the intangibles of making connections. These types of accounts are often devalued or not even considered in schools with a test-driven mentality, especially when those schools are conducting data analysis.

However, for those inquiring about data, other than teacher and student accounts, verifying a positive correlation between "making connections" and measured outcomes, it does exist. Although researchers would recommend against generalizing a causal relationship, our school personnel would differ, because they truly believe the results are attributable to their efforts. Attendance rates are improving at the middle school and high school. Discipline referrals to the office have decreased by 50% at the middle school level and by at least 30% at the high school level. Customer service, relationship building, and making connections with students—including home visits—was the focus of the district for two years prior to a cultural audit. Students are expressing in focus groups that they know someone at school cares about them. Parents share that they feel welcome at school and note that teachers care about their children. The following comments from a recent cultural audit focus group conducted by an external cultural audit team capture some of the thoughts of parents.

Comments and Highlights from 2006 Parent Focus Groups

Primary:

- ☒ "Parents and teachers are talking one on one about progress. This gets results"

- ☒ "I feel comfortable coming to this school."

- ☒ "I moved here and felt welcomed from the start."

- ☒ All parents said there was someone at the school who cared about their child.

- ☒ "I love this school and especially the teachers—they do a great job." (All agreed with this parent's comment.)

☒ All but two parents had received a home visit (One acknowledged that the teacher tried, but they were not there.)

Intermediate:

☒ All parents indicated they felt welcomed when entering the building.

☒ All parents said there was someone at the school who cared about their child.

☒ All parents indicated they had received a home visit.

☒ All parents commented on an environment of enthusiasm.

Middle School:

☒ Parents stated they are treated with great respect; they appreciate what teachers do for the students.

☒ "We didn't get a chance to pick where we live—we were sent here—but we couldn't have asked for a more perfect fit for our child's school. If we could have hand picked, we would have chosen this school."

☒ "Many teachers have provided lifelong memories and had a great impact on students' lives."

☒ "Mrs. Cook (the principal) is great. She even attended a church program to see my child"; "Mrs. Cook always asks about my children"; "I feel I could talk to Mrs. Cook about anything"; "Cook is great!"

☒ All except one parent had received a home visit, and that parent was left a note on the door.

High School:

☒ "Pleased with academics and teachers."

- ☒ "Academics are great—teachers are great."

- ☒ "Many advantages—orchestra, sports, etc."

- ☒ All parents said that at least one teacher had made a strong, positive connection with their child.

- ☒ All parents had received a home visit.

These types of comments from parents may be regarded as "soft" data, but they are qualitative evidence that the efforts and dedication of the staff members are impacting not only parent perceptions about public education, but are making a difference in the lives of their children as well. One should note that parents in the focus group were representative of the demographics at each school.

In addition to feedback on surveys and focus groups, teachers have found some added benefits to home visits. One primary teacher takes a picture of the student's family and then uses that for the seating chart on the first day when students arrive in the classroom. The start of school at the elementary level often begins with a first-day goal of getting students on the right bus to go home. Since teachers have conducted home visits, they know where students live and are no longer perplexed when they hear, "I live in a white house with pink flowers in front of it."

Beyond Home Visits

The Making Connections initiative extends beyond home visits. One of the practices pervasive in Mason County is for the teacher to call a student after the student misses two consecutive days. The purpose is to check on the student, to see if there is anything the school can do, and to simply acknowledge to the student that he or she is missed, and someone is anticipating his or her return to school. At the elementary level, one teacher makes it a practice to call absent students at the same time each day. She holds the phone out to the class, and the rest of the students say in unison, "We miss you!"

Mason County teachers and administrators visit hospitals, provide emotional support to families in crisis, deliver food baskets, deliver homework to absentee students, and ensure that students who want to participate in a school activity can do so without fear of embarrassment or humiliation. The primary school has revised its school supply list so that it does not create an undue financial burden on families. Schools and teachers are seeking and making connections in the classroom and have created classroom binders that depict contacts made between the home and school, as well as information about a student to send to the next grade level so that teachers do not have to start from the beginning each year. Learning profiles, student success plans, and individual learning plans are becoming part of the connections and relationships initiative. All teachers are taking ownership for the students in their classes. The goal is for students to be able to name at least one person at each level who made a difference for them in school.

It's About Expectations and Training

The Making Connections initiative is evident throughout the school district and begins during the interview process with prospective teachers. We have learned that good training cannot help bad hires. Therefore, the district follows the advice of Herb Kelleher at Southwest Airlines in the book *Lessons in Loyalty* by hiring attitude and training skills. It is not an either/or proposition, but a realization that no preservice teacher comes to a school completely prepared to be a master teacher during his or her first years in the classroom. It is the premise of the district that "We can teach and help people develop skills, but we can't teach people to care." Questions during the interview process focus on connections, and the candidate makes a commitment during the interview process they are willing to do home visits.

Once employees are hired, the district has a teacher induction program that anyone new to the district must attend. During this time, mission and goals are addressed, the importance of customer service is emphasized, and teachers receive a copy of a notebook entitled *The Teacher's Backpack.* This is a reference book compiled by district administrators, and one section contains resources for making connections.

Two entries from this section will provide an idea of training materials developed to help teachers improve customer service. The first one is a handout entitled "Exceptional Teacher Customer Service and Public Relations: 29 Ways to Wow Your Parents and Your Administrators!" It seeks to provide teachers with ideas about how they can develop positive relationships with parents and students.

The second handout asks teachers to rate themselves in terms of certain behaviors, and it becomes a tool for self-reflection or for discussion with a colleague or member of the administrative team.

Exceptional Teacher Customer Service and Public Relations
(29 Ways to WOW Your Parents and Your Administrators!)

___1. Make a home visit with parents before the start of the school year. *Find out the gifts of each child, parents' work schedule, and any other pertinent information.*

___2. Make a personal phone call after the first week of school to parents.

  ❑ How was their child's first week of school?

  ❑ Are there any concerns? Are there any questions they need answered?

  ❑ Invite parents to visit your classroom.

___3. Send home handwritten positive notes or postcards throughout the year. Find something positive to say about every child.

___ 4. Review the day's activities at the end of each day so students will have an answer when someone asks, "What did you do in school today?" (*You will need to do this at the end of each class if you teach middle school or high school.*)

___ 5. Give a business card magnet to parents with all important contact information, including appropriate phone numbers and e-mail addresses. Tell them to call you in case of emergency. Let parents know the time of your planning period. ***Respond back to parents within twenty-four hours.***

___ 6. Provide daily/weekly progress reports about students to parents.

___ 7. Help parents fill out necessary forms.

___ 8. Give each parent a brochure about yourself, your degrees and certificates, your hobbies, and what the children will be learning this year. Be sure to include classroom and homework expectations.

___ 9. Find a way to get parents, guardians, and/or grandparents into the classroom to see what has been happening within the classroom. Think about:

     ❑   A showcase of excellence

     ❑   Making your classroom welcoming to volunteers

     ❑   Having meaningful work for parents, guardians, or grandparents to do

___ 10. Invite parents to parent-teacher conference with a personal phone call. Express a genuine interest, and make parents feel welcomed. Treat all parents as if they might be your next school board member. (They might very well be!)

___11. Communicate early and often. Do not wait until conference and report card time to let families know a student is having problems.

___12. Give parents a monthly calendar of events.

___13. Use the *USA Today* philosophy if you are going to send information home: use plenty of pictures and bullets, and limit the words.

___14. Use the school agenda consistently.

___15. Keep an updated Web page.

___16. Keep current with school and district news; people in our community believe you have the "inside word." *(Examples of district documents include: Fast Facts, District Calendar.)*

___17. Frame your diploma and teaching credentials, and hang them up in your classroom. Most professionals proudly display such evidence of their qualifications.

___18. Be positive (always) when you speak about your school and district with families and community members. As far as the community is concerned, you are the school. Your negative comments will reflect on you, especially if they are repeated.

___19. Share with your friends on a regular basis the successes you have with students. These anecdotes will be repeated, too.

___20. Take an active part in your school's parent-teacher organization.

___21. Be friendly and humorous with students. A laugh, pun, wink, or friendly comment can warm relationships and create trust. Be a good listener to students and parents.

____22. Invite senior citizens, business people, legislators, and community leaders to spend time in your classroom as observers, judges, speakers, or volunteers.

____23. Keep your classroom neat and attractive. Paint your room and the halls with quality samples of student work.

____24. Dress as a professional.

____25. Keep confidential information confidential.

____26. Own the parent's question or problem.

____27. Promote a positive partnership with the family. Remember that your students' families are your partners. To promote a partnership, you can:

- Keep a folder for each student's work, which can be sent home, signed by an adult family member, and returned to school.

- Keep a log in your classroom that all children must sign if they fail to do their homework. Have students write in their own words why they failed to do their work. Parents can view the log at any time.

- Have a parent sign homework.

____28. Invite families, and encourage students, to set aside fifteen to twenty minutes each evening for a Family Read-A-Thon. Recognize families that participate.

____29. Keep doing a good job of teaching. That's the best public relations and customer service of all!

Rate Yourself

Rate your parent-teacher conference or your interaction the next time you meet a parent at Wal-Mart, Kroger, or even at school.

____1. Did I project interest and friendliness?

____2. Did I take the initiative in helping solve a particular problem?

____3. Did I use the parent's and student's names at the beginning and end of the exchange?

____4. Was my overall tone positive, with mostly positive word use?

____5. If I am in my classroom, did I get up from behind my desk and sit down with the parent around a table?

____6. Did I listen and let the parent do most of the talking?

____7. Did I show empathy for the parent when it was called for?

____8. Did I avoid using jargon or terms the parent didn't understand?

____9. Did I thank the parent for the opportunity to work with his or her child?

____10. Did I remember that in communication, words only count for 7%; my tone of voice counts for 38%, and body language for 55% of the message I share with parents?

____11. Did I speak positively about the school and school system? If there is a problem, did I own it or pass it to someone else?

Teachers Are at the Heart of the Matter

Schools can have elaborate plans, provide expensive professional development sessions, and have wonderful buildings. When everything is said and done, the variable that matters the most for students and for achievement is the teacher in front of the classroom. The teacher will ultimately determine the future of public education. The person who can help our most disengaged or most promising students realize their potential is the teacher in front of the classroom.

We must now admit that one of the three Rs of schooling is relationships. To this end, we must arm our teachers with awareness and knowledge that developing relationships is critical to the future of students and to public education as we know it, even higher education.

As Brian Nichols, Dean of Education at East Texas Baptist University, shares in a quote from Robert Leeper, "We must remind ourselves that education is a people business (in) which the goals we seek and the things we try must eventually be judged in terms of the persons in the process" (Nichols, 2005).

Teachers are not only the heart of what happens in schools, but they must touch the hearts of the students within their classrooms. Doing so engages the students in learning and lets them know they will be valued for the individuals they are and supported as they travel the sometimes tumultuous road to success. As William Milliken once said, "Programs don't change kids, relationships do ... Nothing matters more to a child than a one-to-one steady relationship with an adult who cares about that child." At this point, it is no longer the Golden Rule but the Platinum Rule that is the true measure of our efforts: *Treat the customer better than we would want our own children treated in schools.*

Chapter Five:

Too Much for One Person

Science assignments often become a long-term project for a student, with the family providing support and encouragement along the way. Such was the case for Devin, who had worked several days collecting and displaying insects for a science project. Devin and his parents were proud of the finished product and could not wait to hear feedback from his middle school science teacher concerning his efforts. Devin barely slept that night in anticipation of his teacher's reaction. The next morning, Devin got dressed, arranged his backpack securely, and carried his collection carefully to the school bus stop.

The bus slowly approached, after making its routine stops along the way, with diesel fumes filling the morning air. As the doors of the bus folded back, Devin, with a smile on his face, carefully lifted his leg to step onto the bus. But before he even reached the first step, he was astonished to hear the bus driver growl in a coarse tone, scowling.

"If you try to bring that bug collection on this bus, I'll throw it out the door. Your bugs will end up in the grass."

Devin could scarcely believe the words ringing through his head. What was he going to do? He backed away from the bus, told the bus driver to go on, and walked dejectedly back to his house.

"Influence may be the highest level of human skills because everything we say and do is the length and shadow of our own souls; our influence is determined by the quality of our being." This thought expressed by Dale Turner reflects the influence each person has whether it's positive or negative. It reflects who we are as human beings. While the importance of the teacher should never be questioned, school districts must procure the assistance of all school personnel in meeting the needs of students. Everyone in the district, every employee has an influence on students. This includes secretaries, cooks, custodians, instructional assistants, and bus drivers. Customer service and making connections with students is a job too big for one person; the service and expertise of all must be enlisted.

The first and last person to see or speak to the majority of students is the bus driver. How the school day begins and ends is in the hands of someone other than the teacher. Think about Devin. His day was ruined, his work was devalued, and his relationship with a school employee created a negative impression of the school district. All the customer service initiatives and all the connections made by the teacher with the student can be negated by the actions of one employee.

What is the implication for school leaders? The response to this question involves broadening the scope of an initiative beyond certified to classified staff and setting forth expectations that support the overall goals and expectations for all employees.

What does customer service look like or sound like for specific job roles? It is evident that training all staff members is critical to success. It is also evident that one must monitor, evaluate, and reward or confront all employees to ensure a high degree of implementation and accountability. Success is greatly enhanced when each group of stakeholders is involved in developing a list of behaviors and expectations for customer service vis-à-vis their positions and duties. As stated previously, the secret is in the creation and customization of ideas for respective schools or districts through the joint efforts of staff members and leaders.

Answers to the question "What does customer service look like or sound like in a particular position?" may vary from district to district. A checklist of ideas for each job description follows. However, these are only examples and should serve as guides as school personnel work collaboratively to develop their own customized list of expectations.

Secretaries: Answering the Call for Customer Service

"Everyone who enters this office must have a higher opinion of the school after they leave than before they came."

Secretaries:

☺ Answer the phone with a smile in their voice

☺ Answer the phone within three rings

☺ Walk visitors to their destination

☺ Are good listeners

☺ Own the problem

☺ Make eye contact with visitors

☺ Are positive about the school and staff to everyone

☺ Maintain a professional environment free of clutter and negative signs

☺ Maintain confidentiality

☺ Make leader aware of problems ahead of time

☺ Redirect phone calls after listening to an issue; if situation is not resolved with person closest to problem or issue, asks person to call back (If problem is with teacher, ask: Have you contacted the teacher? If not, ask them to call the teacher and if they are not satisfied with the outcome to call back)

☺ Screen phone calls for the leader (salespeople, etc.)

☺ Communicate effectively about school, staff, programs, and resources

"Talking it Up" in Transportation

"Too often we underestimate the power of a touch, a smile, a kind word, a listening ear, an honest compliment, or the smallest act of caring, all of which have the potential to turn a life around."

-Leo Buscaglia

Bus drivers:

⊠ Contact the parents of elementary students before school starts.

   * Introduce selves and their bus numbers

   * Explain any important procedures

   * Inquire about any special needs or concerns

   * Share an approximate time to expect the bus

⊠ Get to know the riders on your bus.

   * Use riders' names during conversations.

   * Know about special events in riders' lives.

⊠ Are approachable.

⊠ Greet riders with a smile.

⊠ Encourage riders to have a good day as they exit the bus in the morning.

⊠ Establish procedures and routines related to bus behavior and seating.

⊠ Give administrators a "heads up" when a problem issue has the potential to escalate.

⊠ Provide parents with written directions to an event if driving to an extracurricular event (ballgames, competitions, field trips),

⊠ Maintain a clean and safe environment on the bus.

⊠ Attend training in behavior management when available.

School districts should seek ways to make the customer service initiative a manageable one for bus drivers and transportation workers. One idea that incorporates some of the elements contained within the transportation checklist was developed and implemented on a district-wide basis by the transportation director. During a training session with the transportation personnel, everyone received a copy of a document entitled "Connect Four." It provided a clear explanation of expectations. These involved the expectation that each bus driver would, every month, get to know four riders on their bus route. Drivers recorded information on a sheet monthly, which was monitored by the transportation director.

Making a difference in the lives of students can occur on many different levels. One never knows who might be that one person who connects with a student and provides the encouragement necessary for success. School districts must cast their net of needs and expectations to all employees and use all the time at their disposal. The time to and from school is a valuable time, because it determines how students start and end their day.

Nelson Mandela once asserted, "We must use time wisely and forever realize that the time is always ripe to do right." Without question, what is right is getting to know the students, who take their cue from the people around them. The following pages outline the Connect Four plan and provide a guide for bus drivers in the Making Connections initiative. This is one way school districts can enlist the support and assistance of all employees in reaching out to students.

Connect Four

Remember how good you felt when you connected four ... and won?

We'll be using the slogan of "Connect Four" as we continue

our focus on connecting with kids. Connecting fosters the sense of belonging, which is one of our primary needs.

"Connect" with 4 kids on your bus each month. Target the ones you know least first, and work from there. Put an effort into making the connection significant.

Document your information on the flip side, and develop your file each month, until you have information on all your riders.

Get Connected!

"An optimist is a person who sees a green light everywhere, while the pessimist sees only the red stoplight. The truly wise person is colorblind" (Albert Schweitzer)

Most obvious: Do you know their name?

Do you greet them with a smile and hello each day?

Do you ask about their weekend?

Do you know their favorite thing to do?

Do you listen for clues about their family unit?

Do you tell them to have a good evening or weekend?

Do you know what they want to be when they grow up?

Do you think they feel you are sincere?

Rider: _____
Nickname: _____
Age: _____
Birthdate: _____
School: _____
Favorite thing to do: _____
Who is in their family? _____
_____
What is their favorite subject
in school?_____
What are their plans after sc
hool? _____
_____
Other neat information:_____
_____

Rider: _____
Nickname: _____
Age: _____
Birthdate: _____
School: _____
Favorite thing to do: _____
Who is in their family? _____
_____
What is their favorite subject
in school?_____
What are their plans after sc
hool? _____
_____
Other neat information:_____
_____

My 4 Connections
BUS #:_____

Month:_____

Rider: _____
Nickname: _____
Age: _____
Birthdate: _____
School: _____
Favorite thing to do: _____
Who is in their family? _____
_____
What is their favorite subject
in school?_____
What are their plans after sc
hool? _____
_____
Other neat information:_____
_____

Rider: _____
Nickname: _____
Age: _____
Birthdate: _____
School: _____
Favorite thing to do: _____
Who is in their family? _____
_____
What is their favorite subject
in school?_____
What are their plans after sc
hool? _____
_____
Other neat information:_____
_____

Cooks and cafeteria employees often are underutilized in making connections with students, yet these individuals can help identify students who come to school hungry. When students' basic needs are unmet, the challenge of being successful in school becomes an obstacle course. Observations are only one of many ways cafeteria workers can help connect with students. The following list is a way for administrators to make sure schools are "serving up" good customer service practices.

"Serving Up" Customer Service in the Cafeteria

"To praise is an investment in happiness."

—George Adams

Cafeteria workers:

- Keep the lunchroom clean and smelling good.

- Greet students as they are picking up their trays in line.

- Have fun!

- Compliment students.

- Know students who have limited access to food.

- Sponsor or participate in special events:

    * Lucky trays

    * Cupcakes for birthdays

    * Holidays

- Create an inviting environment in cafeteria (music).

- Try to connect with what's happening in the classroom (spelling words, math facts, etc.).

- Look for ways to help, instead of finding reasons you can't.

Communicating and training the internal public is critical to customer service and to relationship-building in the school. One should never underestimate the importance of the school custodian as a credible source individuals seek out when they want to inquire about the school. Custodians also help insure the upkeep and cleanliness of the building—one of the yardsticks others use to measure the quality of an organization. The following list of attributes of the ideal custodian provides some non-negotiables.

Custodians "Clean-Up" in Customer Service

"Genius is the capacity for seeing relationships where lesser men see none."
–Williams James

Custodians:

- Maintain a neat and clean personal appearance

- Ensure a clean school in all areas, especially bathrooms

- Show pride about work and about responsibilities

- See things that need to be accomplished prior to being told

- Greet visitors in a friendly manner

- Interact positively with students and staff

- Alert administration about possible problems

- Talk positively about the school when in public

- Treat people who rent school facilities in a professional manner

Custodial staff also encounter the public during evening and weekend events, especially when school facilities are rented to organizations, clubs, or groups within the community. Administrators are not always present during these events, during which the public will develop first and lasting impressions of the school and/ or district. One of the tools that can be used to monitor the custodial staff's efforts during such times is the School Event Evaluation Form. When facilities are rented, the rental agreement is accompanied by another form that asks for an appraisal. The custodial staff is aware this is distributed and will be followed up by district and/or school-level administration. The forms are returned to the district office.

Mason County Schools School Event Evaluation Form

We would like for you to take a minute and answer some questions about the service you received while using our facilities.

- Do you feel that the custodian treated you in a courteous, professional manner? Why or why not?

_____

_____

_____

- Did you encounter any problems? If so, what were they?

_____

_____

_____

- What suggestions do you have on how we can make our service better?

_____

_____

_____

Thank you for your time. We hope your experience with Mason County Schools was a positive one.

Relationships are not forged through desire alone. Relationships with students must result from carefully articulated plans that permeate every possible part of school life. Another group of individuals that have a major influence on students are those who wear the title of coach. Students remain connected to schools through their extracurricular experiences. Bonds are formed, life lessons are learned, and students learn about themselves from a coach or sponsor who takes the time to know and develop their skills and interests beyond the school day. Many successful individuals recount the influence of a coach not only in what they learned in a sporting event or club, but in lessons that were transferable to the game of life.

Coaches must hone their customer service skills. Forming positive connections between the student, their families, and the schools can generate a synergy that catapults students to new levels of success. All coaches generate a game plan with the idea of winning. The following suggestions outline a menu of practices that could be useful for helping coaches win the respect and confidence of students and their parents.

Coaching: The Game Plan—

Good Customer Service Practices from Coaches to Parents

1. Get every person affiliated with the team on the same page. Meet with parents before the season starts, and supply an outline of necessary supplies, a game schedule, and a handout of expectations and requirements (such as grade point average, attendance policy, etc.). Develop a list of written expectations for players, and require parents to sign it. The list should also include consequences if expectations are not met.

   a. Conduct parent meeting to go over expectations and rules, and complete all paperwork.

    b. Provide drinks and snacks for parents, and allow them to discuss areas of concern with you.

    c. Conduct this meeting prior to the first practice.

2. Share in advance your desire to communicate with parents, but establish parameters for conversations. Playing time should be an "off-limits" topic. Set aside office hours to hear and address parents' concerns. This allows issues to be settled away from the court or field in an area that is generally calmer. In most circumstances, if parents know that they have a place and time to vent, they will be more satisfied.

3. Address any issues coaches may have with a parent or player in a timely and efficient manner. A coach should not make hasty decisions; at the same time, a coach should never address an issue weeks after he or she becomes aware of it.

4. Communicate to players and to parents that the players are accountable to the program before, during, and after the playing season.

5. Be sure the parents have accurate contact information, so they can get in touch with the coach if they have any questions.

6. Start and end all practices on time. Time is valuable to all people.

7. Get a schedule out early so parents can make plans. Don't wait until the last minute to let parents know about upcoming practices, matches, or games.

    a. Let parents know as soon as possible when a schedule change has occurred.

    b. Provide a weekly or a monthly calendar for players and parents with practice dates and times.

    c. Provide a schedule with alternate location/time for weather/school cancellation prior to beginning practice/training

    d. Have a summer schedule of camps, tournaments, the two-week dead period, and practice schedules after the dead period.

8. Have a place available for parents who want to stay and watch the practice. Don't just push them off to the side. They may want to see how their child is competing. *(Note: If you hold closed practices, make sure to have three to four open practices during the year when parents can observe.)*

9. Send out newsletters to keep parents informed about team events (winter, spring, summer, fall).

10. Provide parents with a schedule that takes them from June 1st until the playoffs.

11. Keep equipment fees as inexpensive as possible.

12. Develop an e-mail distribution list for updates and information relating to the program.

13. Try to have practices and meetings after work hours in the summer so parents can get their kids there.

14. When dealing with younger children, offer a parent clinic (practice with dad/mom) on a Saturday or other convenient time.

15. Have a moms' night to educate mothers about the sport.

16. Conduct monthly parent meetings. Have a focus for each meeting.

17. Learn the names of all of the parents.

18. Host a cookout or other social gathering at the beginning (a get-to-know session) and end of the season (an appreciate-your-support session).

19. Provide a mass physical exam at the fieldhouse for players at a discounted price.

20. Open the high school facility periodically for parents and players in the middle school program.

21. Parents will practice with their children. Practicing a skill the wrong way is worse than no practice at all.

    a. Teach parents some of the basic fundamentals of the game and how you teach each skill.

    b. Sell the parents on teaching the skill the right way. This helps children develop better skills and helps the parent support the coach stress fundamentals.

22. Prepare a weekly practice schedule; give each team member a hard copy, post it on the school Web site, and display it on hallway bulletin boards and in the gymnasium.

23. Publish game schedules in the newspaper, post them at local businesses, broadcast them on the radio, and display individual game dates and times on a signboard.

24. Give parents opportunities for involvement, such as booster clubs, fundraising, and volunteering as referees and coaches.

25. When parents bring items in for concession sales, thank them publicly for their hard work and dedication to the team.

26. Take note of parents who attend and always volunteer to help, and when you order team shirts, order shirts for parents that say, for instance, "Bobbie's Mom."

27. At the end of a sports season, have a picnic or dinner and give out awards not only to the players, but also to the parents. Awards could include: "Yells the loudest for the team," "Raised the most money for uniforms," etc.

28. Let your immediate supervisor know about problems when they arise.

29. Maintain confidentiality and privacy about each student athlete. Do not discuss issues about athletes and/or parents with others on the team.

30. Remain with the players after practice or games until parents arrive.

31. Accentuate the positive in all players, but be honest with students and their parents about roles, skills, and playing time. Don't give false hopes or promises and then not deliver.

32. Establish expectations related to grade point average and behavior, and monitor them throughout the school year, not just during game season.

33. Teach players to leave facilities better than they find them (restaurants, facilities at other schools, hotels, etc).

34. Know the student athletes outside of the gym.

35. Assist parents in completing insurance forms in a timely manner.

36. Implement a phone tree for away games.

37. Provide parents with a written copy of driving directions to the game.

38. Accept blame or fault when something goes wrong, but attribute success to your players, parents, and the school program.

39. Show appreciation to all persons involved in the school program (administrators, teachers, custodians, secretaries).

40. Develop leadership and problem-solving skills among your players.

41. Involve athletes in community service activities.

42. Develop positive relationships with newspaper and radio personnel.

43. Train players in etiquette, communication skills, speaking with the press, and being good ambassadors for the program.

44. Create an honorary coach position for games, or even some practices. This enables school staff or members of the community to observe the realities and the scope of coaching and working with student athletes and might dispel some myths associated with sports programs.

Coaches have to decide on the practices that fit within their philosophy of coaching and within their style. We must realize that coaching, directing, or sponsoring a club requires effective communication with students and their families. One can always expect parents to advocate on behalf of their child, to see a situation from a student perspective, and to be the ears and voices of extracurricular programs. In fact, various programs are often dependent on these individuals, not only for supporting the efforts of their child, but for finding ways to fundraise and become "boosters" for extracurricular activities. Coaches and sponsors should not neglect the role that good customer service can play in their overall program.

The Roll Call Revisited

Who should be excused from a district's roll call in the pursuit of making connections with students? Think about all the staff who could extend their reach to make a difference for students.

Districts must ensure that when roll is taken, all groups are represented and included in helping students be successful in school, through forming positive relationships with students and modeling good customer service practices. Checklists and guides such as those provided throughout this book convey the expectation and foster the practices that customer service, building relationships, and making connections is everyone's responsibility. These checklists encourage all individuals to keep stretching to find ways of achieving better relationships within their various roles in the school. Everyone can make a difference, and everyone can improve their skills in relationship-building and in customer service efforts.

Politicians, parents, and the public often lament the efforts of schools and hold schools and students accountable to ever higher expectations and standards. Calls for rigor must be preceded, or at least accompanied, by the creation of respectful relationships.

In the book *Change Leadership: A Guide to Transforming Our Schools* (2006), the authors maintain that a pivotal element in motivating students to perform at higher levels is quality relationships with their teachers. Regardless of the students' backgrounds and the size of the schools, students in all types of classes "say the one thing that makes the greatest difference in their learning is the quality of their relationships with their teachers" (p.42). One can extend this generalization and make the case that caring relationships that emanate from every employee and permeate every aspect of the school milieu can truly create a learning environment in which all students can do their best. Review the following questions and answers.

Does it sound like common sense?	Yes
Is it easy to do?	No
Does it require everyone to put self-interests aside and focus on what's best for students?	Yes
Will everyone get on board without whining or complaining?	No
Will it happen just because you want it to or because it is a good idea?	No

As one can deduce from the responses, the creation of quality relationships throughout the school requires communication, commitment, and a clear direction for all. A systematic plan involving each of the levels of the school hierarchy must evolve in order to create a culture of quality relationships. We developed the relationship hierarchy below to think about what customer service might look like from one constituent group to another. Utilizing the relationship hierarchy as a guide for establishing expectations offers schools a point of departure for dialogue and for putting their signature on making connections with students.

Relationship Hierarchy Checklist

Among the School Board, Superintendent, and Union	Is there mutual respect and a "no surprises" mentality?
	Are decisions based on what is best for all students?
"Life's most persistent and urgent question is: What are you doing for others?"	Do you actively listen and seek to understand the various perspectives being offered?
	Do you forego personal agendas?
	Do you support the decisions once they are made?
—Martin Luther King, Jr.	Do you convey high expectations and hire, train, and retain the best employees?

	Do you provide support and resources for success?
From the Central Office to School Administration	Do you clearly communicate expectations and provide adequate timelines?
	Do you listen to concerns but maintain a focus on the mission?
"Good leaders make people feel they're at the heart of things, not at the periphery." —Warren Bennis	Do you communicate in words and actions your faith and support of leadership abilities? Do you spend time outside work together?
	Do you praise and celebrate efforts and goals attained? Do you confront and discuss issues that undermine success?
	Do you know professional goals and provide for continued learning opportunities?

	Do you know about your staff's families?
From School Administration to Staff	Do you attend special events, visit staff when they are hospitalized, and express concern?
"A private compliment turned public, instantly and dramatically increases in value." —John Maxwell	Do you recognize staff members for jobs well done?
	Do you provide opportunities for professional growth and leadership, and do you assign staff members based on their areas of strength?
	Do you check on staff when they are absent?

From Staff to Students	Do you make home visits before school starts? Do you call home throughout the year?
"Treat a man as he appears to be and you make him worse. Treat him as if he already were what he could potentially be, and you make him what he should be." —Goethe	Do you know the gifts and talents of your students?
	Do you plant seeds of possibilities and a positive image of what students can attain?
	Do you have high expectations and hold students accountable?
	Do you help create a no-fail culture in your classroom?
	Do you protect the dignity of the learner?

While the checklist is not designed to be all-inclusive, it does offer salient points for discussion as districts seek to customize their working and learning environments to maximize the productive and creative abilities of students and staff. A district or school corporation's relationship hierarchy checklist should reflect their beliefs and priorities as they design a blueprint that will enable each employee to convey, *"Relationships matter!"*

Chapter Six:

Redefining Normal—
Ten Practices to Get There

A*wkward silence filled the air. A young man with widening eyes and a challenging voice complained, "Why should I even try? You don't know anything about me, and you get paid whether I learn or not."*

The faces of the teacher and the principal who witnessed this outburst were bewildered. Both adults were stricken with the sheer honesty of the student's emotion and the veracity of his statement.

This young man's words haunted the principal for weeks to come. While strolling through classrooms, while managing by walking around, while watching with heightened sensitivity the sense of disconnectedness evidenced by many students and even by many of the staff, a gnawing, sick feeling gave way to grave indignation. Questions permeated the principal's thinking.

"How could a school where I am the leader pursue development of relationships with students with such half-heartedness? How might my school dispute the silent claims that the school staff does not care about all students? How might a school act and behave if everyone responded to the silent cries for success and recognition?"

As he continued to engage in this internal dialogue and mulled over his observations, he realized that the actions of the school were in stark contrast to the words contained within the school's mission statement.

As schools, do we ignore the fact that students sometimes feel like mice running on a wheel in a laboratory? Do students believe that education is something done "to" them as opposed to "with" them? What recourse do schools have when the answers to these questions violate the belief system about how schools *should* work?

The answers to these questions have simplistic overtones, but planning, developing, and implementing solutions requires commitment in the face of excuses, relentless determination in the face of opposition to change, and a desire to stay the course in the face of difficult implementation. The transformation from an adult-centered world to one that is student centered will be fraught with naysayers, with roadblocks, and with continued outcries that this is not the school's job. If schools and leaders have resolve, improving schools can occur through systematic efforts in the area of customer service and making connections with students.

In analyzing practices within the business world, we have found in business literature and in corporate practices that customer service practices can inform what schools could be doing. Based on discussions, interviews, and business literature, we have identified a list of ten practices that hold great promise within the educational setting. Along with the ten practices, we have included at least two examples or ideas related to implementation of each practice. School leaders seeking an entry point to making connections and developing relationships among students, parents, staff, and the community can refer to these ten practices as a way of reflecting on where they are and where they want to go. They can also find examples of each practice within their setting. Each school will need to place their fingerprints on the instrument of design and implementation, but at the very least, these ten practices offer talking points for schools, districts, or corporations.

A School's Reference Guide for Customer Service Initiatives

	Practice	Sample Tools
1	Hire the best people and train them.	
	A. Use interview questions for establishing priorities.	* 29 Ways to Wow...
	B. Train all staff, especially front line people.	* Book Study: *The Fred Factor*
2	Collect information about your practices.	
	A. Utilize face-to-face interactions, such as focus groups.	* Cultural Audit
	B. Construct open-ended questions, so individuals can share concerns, offer suggestions for improvement, as well as highlight positive aspects of the school's programs.	* Phone Surveys * Exit Surveys * Customer Feedback Cards
3	Monitor and evaluate performance.	
	A. Incorporate regular status checks. Periodically, use outside sources.	* Pledge Cards
	B. Live by the knowledge that what gets monitored gets done; what gets rewarded gets done.	* Mystery Guest
4	Praise and reward appropriate behavior by spending public relations dollars and time on internal public.	
	A. Spend 90% of public relations dollars on internal staff.	* Fast Facts
	B. Develop special awards that are accompanied by sincere words of praise.	* Personal Awards

5	Make facility maintenance a top priority.	
	A. Use digital camera to capture visual images of: * things that need attention (budget for facility maintenance) * things to praise.	* Event Evaluation Form
	B. Outline and share expectations with staff.	
6	Give great customer service to your employees.	
	A. Communicate with the staff.	* Relationship Hierarchy
	B. Demonstrate in words and actions that you care about the welfare of the staff.	
7	Look for ways to do the "extra" things and to improve customer service.	
	A. Acknowledge and reward staff for out-of-the-box thinking in all aspects of school	* Coaching Game Plan * Pass for Senior Citizens * Birth Packets *Book Discussion: *The Simple Truths of Service Inspired by Johnny the Bagger*
	B. Give staff the authority to make common-sense decisions.	

8	Keep "backstage items" backstage.	
	A. Look at offices, practices, and premises with the customers' eyes. Keep problems out of the public's sight.	
	B. Develop an agreement among councils, staff, board, and committees that the group will not argue in front of the public/media.	
9	Get an A: Acknowledge, Apologize, Affirm.	
	A. Have the expectation and mindset that "We are committed to doing it right the first time."	* Book Study: *One Minute Apology*
	B. Share apology guidelines that include: (1) Offer apology immediately; (2) Make sure apology equals the offense; (3) Be empathetic.	
10	Make connections and form relationships with customers.	
	A. Share rationale on importance of developing relationships with students and parents.	* Best Practice Checklist for Home Visits * Conversation Starters
	B. Commit that all students in the school system will have an advocate who acts on their behalf.	
	C. Train each staff member in making connections.	

These ten practices exemplify what happens within the business world. It can best be described as what the best companies do to become competitive, remain competitive, and enhance their chances of attaining the status of a "great" company. Schools can not only learn from models of the business world but can analyze each of these practices with their own situations in mind.

One disclaimer is that one could spend an entire chapter or even write a book related to each practice. However, the following is meant to offer a quick description of each practice as departure points for rich conversation and discussion as schools seek ways to apply these ideas.

(1) Hire the best people and train them.

From business studies to research studies on schools, the literature indicates that one of the most important practices that distinguishes great organizations from good ones is recruiting, hiring, and then training the best people. In educational research, the work of Katie Haycock and others relates how student achievement is impacted by teacher quality. In business literature, companies such as Southwest Airlines point to their practice of attracting the best people to their company as a catalyst for their success in an ever-demanding and changing industry.

Schools must examine their efforts in terms of recruiting, hiring, training, and retaining the best teachers and the best staff members. The hiring process must be divorced from political pressures, from the idea of local hires, and from looking at the school as an employment agency. The hiring process must be married to the ideas of attracting the best candidate, establishing expectations within the interview process, and determining what individual best meets the demands of the position and will nurture students throughout their educational career.

Once an individual is employed, schools must provide resources and personnel to support the efforts of the new employee. Teacher induction programs are critical to the continuing growth and development of someone who is new to teaching or to the district or school system. Retaining the best personnel is more likely when new employees feel connected to the school system, knowing that resources and other professionals are easily accessible. As schools seek to train employees on the importance of customer service and making connections, the book *The Fred Factor* by Mark Sanborn can be a great resource for initiating discussions about how each employee can become a "Fred." The book offers many salient practices and ideas by describing Fred, a postal worker who was valued by others because of the way he treated them. A "Fred" is an ordinary person who gives extraordinary service to others because he simply enjoys it. Random acts of goodness characterize the efforts of anyone who desires to become a "Fred." The book outlines principles and ways organizations can seek out and develop Freds among their employees.

(2) Collect information about your practices.

Schools have a tendency to view their practices based on their good intentions, rather than how their practices may be viewed by the customers or the general public. Access to perceptions and to insights about how schools do business offers great opportunities for improving services and leads to the implementation of effective, efficient customer service practices. Schools must devise questions with the intent of acquiring a realistic portrayal of the school's practices. These questions should be open ended and allow respondents to honestly take a path that reflects their experiences and perceptions. Additionally, questions should incorporate the district's current efforts to assess how these practices are viewed by the different stakeholders. Skewing the questions, omitting topics, or being defensive within group discussions negates the impact this information can yield.

Chapter three offers a detailed explanation of obtaining information about the school's practices through cultural audits, focus groups, telephone surveys, and the like. In order for this information gathering to be effective, schools must first negotiate internally the tendency to "explain away" negative results or to "put a new coat of paint over a bad spot on the wall." Collecting information must be accompanied by a desire to address the issues that may arise. Schools must then be prepared to prioritize the efforts needed, especially when they involve forming positive relationships with all students and their families.

(3) Monitor and evaluate performance.

Organizations typically excel in deciding on an initiative and implementing it, but they then drop the ball when it comes to monitoring and evaluating its status or effectiveness. Unfortunately, leaders often have a mental to-do checklist; once the initial implementation occurs, a checkmark is made to the left of the item, and few contemplate the next steps or even consider the question: "How will we know this is working or having the expected outcome?"

The barometers used to measure such ideas could be referred to as belly barometers—"It's just a gut feeling, but I think everything is going fine." Such measures do not lead to productive implementation, and they allow people and practices to fall through the cracks. There must be measurable outcomes and frequent status checks about where one is in the implementation process or where performance has improved. These must be demystified, deliberate, discussed, and debated to insure progress. One of the most difficult mental tasks is simplifying complex ideas so others can see that goals are attainable with intentional actions and frequent feedback. Goals must be clear, communicated, and coordinated within the school setting. Everyone must know that the goals are important enough to the leader that there will be follow-up and that there is a systematic process in place for monitoring and evaluating the overall impact of an initiative, practice, or even individual performance.

One strategy often utilized in the business community is the "mystery guest." Schools can employ this strategy as well. Phone calls or visits to schools by "pretend" prospective parents provide a realistic example of how customers are treated in the school system. One can arm mystery guests with questions about programs and services, and this provides an effective way to monitor and evaluate customer service efforts.

Our school district has employed this strategy; we have solic-
ited individuals to become mystery guests at one of our schools,
pretending to enroll a child, asking questions about the school, and
then sharing their experience with district personnel. Again, this
information is used to praise individuals for their interaction with
the mystery guest or to address areas where we could improve.

(4) Praise and reward appropriate behavior.
   The desire for praise and recognition rivals some of life's other
important desires. The best companies realize that employee performance and productivity are directly tied to recognizing the efforts
of employees who adhere to the organization's values. The Yum
Corporation in Louisville, Kentucky, which boasts such recogniz-
able brands as Kentucky Fried Chicken, Taco Bell, Pizza Hut, A
& W, and Long John Silvers, is one of the premier companies in
praising and recognizing employees for customer service efforts.
In fact, Ken Blanchard wrote the book *Customer Mania* to high-
light the efforts of this company. Employee recognition is one of
the hallmarks of Yum and is prevalent through personalized notes
and symbols showcasing the commitment of all involved. The Yum
Corporation executives maintain that recognition doesn't have to
cost a great deal.
   Southwest Airlines executives share the same view in the book
Lessons in Loyalty. Each corporation shares the importance of simple, genuine, and ongoing acknowledgement of the efforts of staff
who demonstrate that they care about the customer. These corporations emphasize the power of "in-the-moment" recognitions, as
opposed to ones conducted at the end of the year.
   Schools would do well to embrace this practice, which is often
regarded by some school leaders as too "touchy-feely" to have any
real significance for school improvement. The concept of praising
and rewarding behavior is often negated by some as an expendable
dimension in the litany of things on the to-do list. However, the fallacy of these assumptions leads one down a slippery slope of unreal-
ized expectations. Leaving out incentives results in change coming
at a much slower pace than could be achieved. with their inclusion.

(5) Make facility maintenance a top priority.

Appearance is the most common denominator in making judgments about people and places. Judgments are rendered rather quickly and are often difficult to change in the court of public opinion. Everyone can identify with the experience of going to a restaurant or another public place and instantaneously forming an impression about the quality of the establishment based on its cleanliness. The same is true with public schools. Restrooms tell the story when it comes to cleanliness and upkeep, and one can be sure that almost every person will frequent the restroom. Individuals who visit campuses and who attend school functions have an opinion about schools and school leadership based on facility maintenance and upkeep. Schools should strive to keep their facilities looking like Disney World.

However, not everyone has the same standards of quality and excellence. One must also acknowledge that habitually being somewhere has a tendency to blind one to the eyesores that might exist within a building or on school grounds. A set of fresh eyes can often uncover and pinpoint problem areas. There must be an expectation that cleanliness and upkeep are everyone's responsibility, not just the custodial staff's. Schools should annually budget funds related to improving school facilities.

(6) Give great customer service to employees.

Leaders must make sure they don't utilize a parent-child relationship with staff. It is so easy to fall in the trap of "Do as I say" versus "Watch what I do." However, one of the most powerful methods of influence is modeling the behavior you expect from others. One cannot expect staff members to reach out and put forth the extra effort if the leader is unwilling to do the same for their staff. While leaders cannot be "friends" with staff members, they can demonstrate they care about each person through their interactions, by listening, by checking on staff members who are sick, by attending important events in the lives of their staff members.

One of the most overlooked aspects of providing good customer service to staff is through effective communication. A level of frustration permeates schools where information is funneled through the grapevine and an array of channels, as opposed to direct communication with the staff. Often the "what" and the "how" are conveyed without the benefit of the "why." Leaders must be deliberate in their efforts to communicate with the staff and make sure they have accurate information.

(7) Look for ways to do the "extra" things and to improve customer service.

It has been said that there is only one degree of difference between hot water and boiling water. It's the little things that make a huge difference for parents. It just takes a little more effort and thought about how we can make things better for our customers. What can the school do to make a situation easier for parents? Is there someone to assist with the paperwork?

Find the special things staff members are doing for students and/or their parents, and recognize their efforts. Schools can brainstorm a variety of ideas about how to do the extras. Our district embraces the concept of education from "womb to tomb" and seeks ways to develop relationships by providing the extras. Parents of newborn children in the district receive a birth packet with a onesie that reads, "Future Graduate of Mason County Schools," the book *Goodnight Moon* by Margaret Wise Brown, and other developmental literature and checklists.

We have a picture identification, the "Royal Pass," for senior citizens, which enables them to come to athletic events for free and to attend musicals and other school events for half price. As the baby boomer population ages, it is estimated that 75% of citizens in a community do not have any children in schools. The Royal Pass is one way we honor this population and seek to involve these valued members of the community in school-related activities. It also provides the district with a database of this constituency to help plan future events geared toward this audience. Other examples of doing the extras might include:

⊠ Customer service ideas from coaches to parents

⊠ Driving directions to off-campus sites for school events

⊠ Inviting businesses and organizations to conduct their meetings at our school facilities

⊠ Packets of color-coded notes with all forms parents might need; parents fill in the blanks (Absences; riding a different bus; lunch notes; services requested)

⊠ An established process for enrolling new students with assistance to parents for paperwork and follow-up phone calls to the home within the first two days to inquire about concerns

(8) Keep backstage items backstage.

Keeping backstage items backstage is a concept utilized by David Reed and David Cottrell in the book *Monday Morning Customer Service*. The authors note: "Backstage refers to things behind the scenes where the customer does not see or hear them" (Reed & Cottrell, 2004, p. 113). Schools are notorious for putting problems front and center. As one enters the office at school, one might see students who are ill, students who are upset, students who are waiting for disciplinary actions, or even students who have lice. Schools need to think about ways of addressing their students' needs without the public spectacle that typically accompanies the school waiting room. The office needs to be a welcoming place where customers are exposed to a positive atmosphere free of clutter, problems, and unfolding dramas.

Additionally, meetings of the school board, committees, site-based councils, Parent Teacher Association meetings open up opportunities for negative comments in a public forum. Within the school community and among professionals, disagreements and discussions should occur behind closed doors, especially discussions where it is evident that the wagons are being circled and people are shooting inward. Everyone walks away from these types of encounters with a negative impression of the school and often the employees. Positive conflict, where individuals are focused on examining different sides of an issue, is productive when conducted in an atmosphere of trust and where everyone is acting on what is best for the school, free from individual agendas. There needs to be an atmosphere of mutual respect where professionals can agree to disagree in an amicable way without finger-pointing and arguing in public. The establishment of ground rules can be useful in these situations, as well as adhering to General Colin Powell's philosophy:

> When we are debating an issue, loyalty means giving me your honest opinion, whether you think I'll like it or not. Disagreement, at this stage stimulates me. But once a decision has been made, the debate ends. From that point on, loyalty means executing the decisions as if they were your own (Quote DB, 2007, p. 1).

Keeping backstage items backstage, with the knowledge that the group will have the opportunity to voice opinions, share concerns, and develop solutions helps maintain an atmosphere of respect and professionalism. It also keeps those who love chaos from having the opportunity to create more of it.

(9) Get an A: Acknowledge, Apologize, Affirm.
No organization is mistake free, yet defensiveness is usually the first reaction when someone within an organization is contacted about a problem or issue. Mistakes in judgment, errors in recording information, misspoken words—these happen everywhere, even in schools. The issue is not whether we make mistakes, because we do; the issue is how we react or recover from those mistakes, as unintentional as they may be. Avoidance and defensiveness must be replaced by a willingness to listen and an assurance that someone from the school system will inquire and find out the facts in any given situation.

In an article entitled "Ten Customer Service Secrets to Win Back Customers," Ed Sykes suggests one of the most important things a person can do when told of a problem is to smile and introduce himself as someone who will help solve the problem. From the examples provided in the article, an educator might begin with a starter such as:

"Hello, my name is _____. I am the _____ *(role)* for _____ *(school)*. I am here to assist you in this situation. Please tell me about it."

Key to this process is intently listening to the other person. Words and actions during this initial discussion will either escalate or de-escalate the situation. Sykes provides some dos and don'ts related to listening. They include:

Do:

- Listen with an open mind.

- Think about the dilemma from the other person's perspective.

- Use statements such as:

    o   I can appreciate what you're saying.

    o   I can see how you'd feel that way.

    o   I can see how you'd be upset.

    o   It sounds as if we've caused you inconvenience.

    o   What I understand the situation to be is …

Don't:

- Appear hostile or inconvenienced .

- Alienate the person more with statements such as:

    o   I don't know why you are so upset.

    o   That's the first complaint we ever got on that.

    o   I know how you feel.

o   Boy, you're sure mad

(Sykes, 2005, p. 3)

There are at least two sides to every situation, and it is incumbent that decision-making be predicated on getting all the facts from the different stakeholders. Once the facts are learned, and if staff members or the school is found to be at fault, then individuals must be contacted, the situation explained, and a genuine apology offered. The book, *The One Minute Apology* offers specific guidelines about offering apologies. Three key concepts from this book are instrumental in recovering from mistakes. They include:

(1) Offer the apology immediately. The more time that elapses between the offense and the apology, the more emotional the offended party becomes, and the less likely that the apology will seem genuine.

(2) The apology must equal the offense. If someone was publicly humiliated, a public apology is required.

(3) Be empathetic with the offended individual(s). Think how you would respond and how you would want to be treated in the same situation.

Schools must be willing to acknowledge when they make mistakes, apologize in an appropriate manner, and affirm to the injured party that he or she is valued and the mistake will not be repeated. Great leaders can save the day, and most people are willing to forgive if the situation is handled appropriately, in a timely manner, and with sincerity. The best defense against accusations and mistakes in judgment within the school environment is a history of all staff members being committed to doing things right the first time and the knowledge that everyone is treated fairly and with respect, and that the school is willing to listen.

(10) Make connections and form relationships with the customers.

John Dewey once stated that what the best and wisest parents want for their own child should be what the educational community wants for all its children. If one had the opportunity to inquire from these "wise parents" what their wants would be in relation to their child's educational career, some nonnegotiables would be that the school: knows their child, nurtures the gifts and abilities of their child, and engages their child with a challenging and relevant curriculum. The teacher-student relationship is paramount to the success of all students, especially those from poverty.

As mentioned earlier, the book *Change Leadership:A Practical Guide to Transforming Our Schools*, underscores the importance of schools developing practices around making connections and forming relationships with students. The authors write:

> The most important element in motivating students to want to achieve at high standards: the quality of relationships with their teachers. It has always been true that students tend to learn very little from teachers who they feel are not respectful toward them. They may feel goaded into doing the minimum by a teacher who uses fear and intimidation, but they will never do their best even in subjects they enjoy. And for today's students, who often have little contact with their parents or other adults, relationships with caring, respectful teachers have become even more important (Wagner et al., 2006, p. 42).

Wagner and his colleagues support this position based on research and focus group surveys with students. Student responses to questions contain valuable information for the educational community, informing practitioners that schools must begin their journey toward continuous improvement by focusing on developing relationships with students. The results should guide the work of educators. Consider the following:

Students attending urban, suburban or rural high schools; students who struggle academically; and students who take advanced courses all say the one thing that makes the greatest difference in their learning is the quality of their relationships with their teachers. They want teachers who care about teaching and who are challenging, competent, of course, but what they talk about most often is how they are treated by their teachers. Does the teacher see them as individuals, rather than just faces in the crowd? Does the teacher try to know and understand what students may be dealing with at home or in their neighborhood? To what extent does a teacher go out of his or her way to ensure that all students are learning versus just plowing through the chapters? Or does the teacher only pay attention to the "smart" kids? It is increasingly clear to us that, although many of today's students may have diminished fear and respect for formal authority, they have an increased need to connect with adults who can guide and coach them in school and in life (p. 42–43).

How can schools foster these connections and develop positive relationships between teachers and students? Home visits are a great tool to be utilized in the process, but they are just the tip of the iceberg when it comes to actually developing positive relationships with students. One might begin by sharing with staff members a rationale for developing relationships with students and parents. Information and statistics contained in chapters two and four provide resources for developing this rationale. Secondly, schools must make the commitment that each student in the school system will have an advocate who acts on his or her behalf. "Somebody for me" is the assurance students should expect from schools. "Somebody for me" is a person who challenges students and holds them to high expectations. "Somebody for me" is the teacher who serves as a primary support system. Students will be successful if they truly believe the adults at school care about them and are there to be their advocate. Finally, train each staff member in making connections, and monitor those efforts. As unbelievable as it might sound, there are several professionals within the educational community who are nervous, uncomfortable, or unsure about "this relationship-building thing," or those who simply believe they are there strictly to teach content. Educators must heed the words of Carl Jung, who advised as follows:

> An understanding heart is everything for a teacher, and cannot be esteemed highly enough. One looks back with appreciation to the brilliant teachers, but with gratitude to those who touched our human feeling. The curriculum is so much necessary raw material, but warmth is the vital element for the growing plant and for the soul of the child (The Quotations Page, 2007, p. 1)

One must note that having an understanding heart does not mean eliminating rigor from the curriculum. In fact, building connections with students makes it possible to ensure that all students have access to what Mike Schmoker, deemed a guaranteed and viable curriculum. Schools can expect more from students when relationships have been forged, safety nets have been developed, and progress is being monitored by someone who truly cares about the student. The poet Longfellow noted that "The heart has its own memory," and schools would do well to remember this.

The School's Modus Operandi (M.O.)

As one reflects about how schools operate, one thing becomes evident: business as usual must be challenged if relationships are not the foundational piece of school improvement. We must constantly search within ourselves, with other schools, and with students to *redefine normal*. Normal in many schools is not working. Normal is not producing the results that are possible within the educational setting. Normal is just another way of remaining at status quo, an excuse that is used to resist change. Schools can no longer afford to massage and manipulate the reality of their circumstances, of their shortcomings, of their failures, especially the reality of disengagement and distance that characterizes so many students. Redefining normal offers hope to public education, promise to its youth, and growth to its employees. Redefining normal means that schools seize the opportunity to assess ways they can intentionally and systemically foster positive relationships between the students and the staff. Redefining normal means that schools must incorporate customer service practices in meeting the needs of parents, students, and the community. Normal is no longer good enough.

One writer and philosopher exemplified the idea of redefining normal in the world of children's literature. The words of Dr. Seuss remind us about where the challenge of redefining normal must begin:

> **UNLESS** someone like you cares a whole awful lot, Nothing is going to get better, it's not. (*The Lorax*, p. 58)

School leaders and professionals who embrace the educational process as an important roadmap to success for all students must demonstrate through words and actions that we care "a whole awful lot," even if it is one person at a time. Customer service, developing relationships, and making connections are the linchpens to changing the negative direction characterizing so many public schools. The words of Dr. Seuss must ring in our ears—"Nothing is going to get better, it's not"—until we care "a whole awful lot."

"A Little Extra" Appendix

Quotations on Relationships

No significant learning occurs without a significant relationship.

—Dr. James Comer

Every master teacher seeks "chemistry" with students.

—J. Brian Nichols

Two factors which help one leave poverty: education and a key relationship.

—Ruby Payne

The driving forces for decision making are survival, relationships, and enjoyment.

—Ruby Payne

If you can show me how I can cling to that which is real to me, while teaching me into the larger society, then I will not only drop my defenses and my hostility, but I will sing your praises and I will help to make the desert bear fruit.

—Ralph Ellison, The Invisible Man

Children do not care how much you know until they know how much you care.

—Ruby Payne

Only when learning occurs, does teaching happen.

—Ruby Payne

We must neither excuse them nor scold them; we must teach them.

—Ruby Payne

Research shows us that the successful development of language occurs with supportive, positive and encouraging relationships.

—Martin and Pat Buoncristiani

Learning is only possible after a student's social, emotional and physical needs have been met.

—Council on Adolescent Development

Children's most meaningful learning occurs through positive and supportive relationships with caring and nurturing adults.

—Dr. James Comer

To live in a quantum world, we need to change what we do. We need to stop describing tasks and instead facilitate a process. We need to become savvy about how to build relationships and learn how to nurture growing and changing things. We will need better skills in listening, communicating, and facilitating groups, for these are the talents that build strong communities.

—Margaret Wheatley

I put the relationship of a fine teacher to a student just below the relation of a mother to a son.

—Thomas Wolfe

The primary motivator of whether kids in poverty will learn is whether they like the teacher. It's that relationship. It comes down to two things: you've got to teach them how to live in a paper world, and you have to have a relationship of respect with them.

—Ruby Payne

Programs don't change kids, relationships do ... nothing matters more to a child than a one-to-one steady relationship with an adult who cares about that child.

—William E. Milliken

This is the value of the teacher, who looks at a face and says there's something behind that and I want to reach that person, I want to influence that person, I want to encourage that person, I want to enrich, I want to call out to that person who is behind that face, behind that color, behind that language, behind that tradition, behind that culture: I believe you can do it. I know what was done for me.

—Maya Angelou

The greatest accolade a teacher can receive is when a student says, "I like me when I'm with you."

—Marva Collins

References

Alt, M. N., & Peter, K. (2002, September 5). *Findings from the condition of education 2002: Private schools—A brief portrait.* Washington DC: National Center for Educational Statistics. Retrieved May 3, 2005, from http://nces.ed.gov/programs/coe/2002/analyses/private/sa01c.asp

Anonucci, M. (2001, September 1). NEA members rate vouchers "Not important." *School Reform News.* 1–3. Retrieved January 17, 2007, from http://www.heartland.org/Article.cfm?artId=10204

Black, J., & English, F. (1986). *What they don't tell you in schools of education about school administration.* Lancaster, PA: Technomic.

Blanchard, K., & Glanz, B. (2005). *The simple truths of service inspired by Johnny the bagger.* San Diego, CA: Blanchard Family Partnerships.

Blanchard, K., & McBride, M. (2003). *The one minute apology: A powerful way to make things better.* New York: Harper Collins Publisher

Blanchard, K., Ballard, J., & Finch, F. (2004). *Customer mania: It's never too late to build a customer focused company.* New York: Free Press.

Blankstein, A. (2004). *Failure is not an option: Six principles that guide student achievement in high performing schools.* Bloomington, IN: The HOPE Foundation

Bracey, G. (2004). *The seven deadly absurdities of No Child Left Behind Legislation.* Retrieved January 16, 2006, from http://nochild;eft.com/2004/oct04absurd.html

Brainy Quotes. Retrieved July 14, 2007, from http://www.brainy-quote.com/quotes/quotes/f/fscottfit403120.html

Brandt, R. (2002, April). The case for diversified schooling. *Educational Leadership, 59*(7), 12–19.

Brondos, J. A. (2004, September 23). Public school no place for teachers' kids. *Washington Times.* Retrieved May 3, 2005, from http://joelbrondos.worldmagblog.com/joelbrondos/archives/008929.html

Brown, R. (2004). School culture and organization: Lessons from research and experience. A background paper for the Denver Commission on secondary school reform. Retrieved July 15, 2007, from http://www.dpsk12.org/pdf/culture_organization.pdf

Caire, K. (2002, April). The truth about vouchers. *Educational Leadership, 59*(7), 38–42.

Cloud, D. (2004, June 30). *The Southern Baptist convention and the public school system.* Retrieved May 12, 2005, from http://www.wayoflife.org/fbns/sbc-homeschool.html

Clark, R. (2003). *The essential 55.* New York: Hyperion

Clowes, G. (2000, August). Double standard on school choice. *School Reform News.* Heartland Institute. Retrieved May 3, 2005, from http://www.heartland.org/Article.cfm?artID=10939

Clowes, G. (2001, July 1). Is unionization of teachers good for students? *School Reform News.* Heartland Institute. Retrieved January 17, 2007, from http://www.heartland.org/Article.cfm?artID=9912

Collins, J. (2001). *Good to great why some companies make the leap ... and others don't.* New York: Harper Business.

Comer, J. P. (2004). *Leave no child behind: Preparing today's youth for tomorrow's world.* New Haven, CT: Yale University Press

Committee on Increasing High School Students' Engagement and Motivation to Learn & National Research Council (2003). *Engaging schools: Fostering high school students' motivation to learn.* National Academies Press. Retrieved July 3, 2006, from http://www.nap.edu/openbook/0309084350/html/14.html

Corbett, D., & Wilson, B. (2002, September). What urban students have to say about good teaching. *Educational Leadership, 60*(1), 18–22.

Deiro, J. (2003, March). Do your students know you care? *Educational Leadership, 60*(6), 60–62.

Duin, J. (2004). Southern Baptists eye exiting public schools. *The Washington Times.* Retreived May 12, 2005, from http://www.washtimes.com/national/20040511-111759-5766r.htm

Feller, B. (2004, August 4). "Home schooling rises as parents seek peace of mind, academic control," *The Ledger Independent.* Maysville, KY p. A11

Fitzwater, I. (1996). *Time management for school administrators.* Rockport, MA: ProActive

Fredericks, J. A., Blumfield, P.C., & Paris, A. H. (2004). School engagement: Potential of the concept, state of the evidence. *Review of Educational Research, 74*(1), 59–109.

Geisel, T. S. (1971). The lorax by Dr. Seuss. New York, NY: Random House.

Georgiades, W., Fuentes, F., & Snyder, K. (1983) *A meta-analysis of productive school cultures.* Houston: University of Texas.

Gipson, C. (2002, August 1). Washington state think tank takes on the NEA—Will court let teachers halt NEA politicking with their money? *Labor Watch.* 1–7. Retrieved January 17, 2007, from http://www.heartland.org/Article.cfm?artID=1210

Grubbs-West, L. (2005). *Lessons in loyalty: How Southwest Airlines does it—An insider's view.* Dallas, TX: Cornerstone Leadership Institute.

Haycock, K. (2006, September). *Gaining traction in our high schools: Critical leverage points for superintendents.* Education Trust. Presentation, Lexington, KY.

Heifetz, R., & Linsky, M. (2002). *Leadership on the line: Staying alive through the dangers of leading.* Boston: Harvard Business School Press.

Hess, F., & West, M. (2005, April 5). A better bargain overhauling teacher collective bargaining for the 21st Century. Retrieved July 9, 2007, from http://www.ksg.harvard.edu/pepg/PDF/Papers/BetterBargain.pdf

Hirsh, S. (2002, May). Make equity a priority. National Staff Development Council. Retrieved January 19, 2007, from http://www.nsdc.org/library/publications/results/res5-02hirs.cfm

Holloway, J. H. (2002, April). For-profit schools. *Educational Leadership, 59*(7), 84–85.

Home School Legal Defense Association. (2007, July). *State laws.* Retrieved July 5, 2007, from http://www.hslda.org/laws/default.asp

Howe, K., Eisenhart, M., & Betebenner, D. (2002, April). The price of public school choice. *Educational Leadership, 59*(7), 20–24.

Hunter, B. (2004, June 30) *Effective advocacy for public education: What has AASA learned so far?* Louisville, KY: Presentation at Kentucky Association of School Superintendents.

Hunter, B. (2005, September 30). *What's up in Washington?* Retrieved July 9, 2007, from http://smartedu.org/nhsaa/forms/2004

Indiana University (2005). *2005 High school survey of student engagement: What we can learn from high school students.* Bloomington, IN: Indiana University. Retrieved July 3, 2006, from www.iub.edu/~nsse/hsse

Irvine, M. (2007). Montgomery Ward shutting down after 125 years. *The Berkeley Daily Planet.* Retrieved January 16, 2007, from http://www.berkeleydailyplanet.com

Joy, J. (2006). How to be a customer-focused company. Retrieved July 9, 2007, from http://ezinearticles.com/?how-to-be-a-customer-focused-company

Kinnaman, D. E. (2007, July). Roosevelt vs. Reagan ... and the future of public education in the United States. *District Administration*, 72.

Klein, K. (2007, June). *Building customer relations by listening*. http://www.businessweek.com/smallbiz/content/jun2007/sb20070601_858776.htm?campaign_id=rss_daily [July 9, 2007]

Klem, A., & Connell, J. P. (2004, September). Relationships matter: Linking teacher support to student engagement and achievement. *Journal of School Health*. 262–273.

Leland. K., & Bailey, K. (1999). *Customer service for dummies*. Chicago, IL: IDG Books Worldwide Inc.

Lubienski, C., & Lubienski, S. (2004, December). Re-examining a primary premise of market theory: An analysis of NAEP data on achievement in public and private schools."Retrieved May 7, 2005, from http://www.ncspe.org/publications_files/OP102.pdf

Maciejewski, J. (2007, July). Broadening collective bargaining. *District Administration*, 35–39.

Maranto, R. (2002, August/September). AFT charter school "study" lobbying, not research. *National Charter School Clearinghouse News*. Retrieved May 20, 2005, from http://www.ncsc.info/newsletter/August_September_2002/AFT_Response.htm

Mason County Student Focus Groups (2006, May). Maysville, KY.

Maxwell, J. (2005). *The 360 degree leader developing your influence from anywhere in the organization*. Nashville, TN: Thomas Nelson.

McDonald, T. (2002, April). The false promise of vouchers. *Educational Leadership, 59*(7), 33–37.

Moe, T. (2001). A union by any other name. *Education next—A journal of opinion and research*. Retrieved May 20, 2005, from http://www.educationnext.org/20013/38moe.html

Monroe, L. (1999). *Nothing's impossible: Leadership lessons from inside and outside the classroom*. New York: Public Affairs.

Motivational quotes. Retrieved May 4, 2005, from (http://www.famous.motivational-quotes.com/motivational-story-7.html)

Mowbray, J. (2001, November). The NEA's political machine new evidence indicates misuse of tax exempt dues. The Labor Watch. Washington DC: Capital Research Center. 1–7. Retrieved January 17, 2007, from http://www.heartland.org/Article.cfm?artId=8808

National Research Council. (2003). Engaging schools: Fostering high school students' motivation to learn. Washington, DC: National Academies Press.

Nichols, J. B. (2005, February 15). Improving Academic Performance through the enhancement of teacher student relationships: The relationship teaching model. Chicago, IL: Association of Teacher Educators.

Payne, R. K. (2001). *A framework for understanding poverty*. Highlands, TX: aha! Process, Inc.

Payne, R. K. (2006, January/2005, December). Understanding poverty. *Compensatory Education Programs & Title I, 3*(5). Winston-Salem, NC: Winston-Salem/Forsyth County Schools

Quote DB. Retrieved July 14, 2007, from (http://www.quotedb.com/authors/elbert-hubbard/2)

Quote DB. Retrieved July 14, 2007, from (http://www.quotedb.com/quotes/1051)

Ray, B. (2002, April). Customization through homeschooling. *Educational Leadership, 59*(7), 50–54.

Reed, D., & Cottrell, D. (2004). Monday morning customer service. Dallas, TX: Cornerstone Leadership Institute

Reeder, S. (2005). Local influence adds to teacher-union power. Small Newspaper Group Springfield Bureau. Retrieved January 19, 2007, from http://thehiddencostsoftenure.com/stories/?prcs s=display&id=266550

Reich, R. (2002, April). The civil perils of homeschooling. Educational Leadership, 59(7), 56–59.

Sagor, R. (2002, September). Lessons from skateboarders.Educational Leadership, 60(1), 34–38.

Sanborn, M. (2004). The Fred factor. New York: Doubleday

Schlechty, P. (2005) Creating great schools. San Francisco, CA: John Wiley & Sons.

Schmmoker, M. (1999). Results: The key to continuous improvement. Alexandria, VA: ASCD.

Sykes, E. (2005, May 11). Ten customer service secrets to win back customers. Retrieved July 9, 2007, from http://searchwarp.com/swa8006.htm

Talaski, K. (2001). How the mighty department store has fallen. W Retrieved August 15, 2007, from (http://www.mailarchive.com/penl@galaxy.csuchico.edu/msg51866.html)

Teacher unions. Retrieved May 20, 2005, from (http://www.ncsc.info/newsletter/August_September_2002/AFT_Resp   onse.htm

The Quotations Page. Retrieved July 14, 2007, from (http://www.quotationspage.com/quote/9787.html)

Thinkexist Quotations. Retrieved July 14, 2007, from (http://thinkexist.com/quotations/perception/

Thinkexist Quotations. Retrieved July 14, 2007, from http://thinkexist.com/quotation/strange_is_our_situation_here_upon_earth-each_of/8534.html

Thomas, R. (2001). Rethinking shopping. Retrieved August 15, 2007, from (http://www.mail-archive.com/penl@galaxy.csuchico.edu/msg51866.html)

Tomlinson, C. A. (2002, September). Invitations to learn. *Educational Leadership*, *60*(1), 6–10.

Turner, R.F. (2003, March). Fact sheet understanding poverty: An overview. Retreived August 21, 2007, from (http://www.ext.wvu.edu/cyfar/rut/fact%20sheet%20)

Voices of Reason Student Summit, (2006). Shepherdsville, KY: Kentucky Department of Education

Wagner, T., Kegan, R., et al. (2006). *Change leadership A practical guide to transforming our schools*. San Francisco, CA: Jossey-Bass

Walsh, M. W. (2006, November 6). Once safe, public pensions are now facing cuts.*New York Times*. Retrieved January 16, 2007, from http://www.nytimes.com/2006/11/06/business/06pension.html

Willingham, R. (1992). *Hey, I'm the customer: Front line tips for providing excellent customer service*. Upper Saddle River, NJ: Prentice Hall

Willis, S. (2002, April). Customization and the common good, a conversation with Larry Cuban. *Educational Leadership*, *59*(7), 6–11.

Wong, H., & Wong, R. (2001). *The first days of school—How to be an effective teacher*. Mountain View, CA: Harry K. Wong Publications.

Made in the USA
San Bernardino, CA
10 August 2013